Vocabulary Power
Through Shakespeare

Essential Words for Reading Comprehension,
Writing, Speech, and Standardized Examinations

David Popkin

Other books by David Popkin:
Vocabulary Energizers
Vocabulary Energizers II

ISBN 0-929166-03-5

First Printing: October 2002.
Second Printing: April 2003

Printed in the United States of America

Hada Publications
2605 Belmont Boulevard
Nashville, TN 37212

Contents

DEDICATION

For my children Dan, Joan, and Phil

Introduction

Shakespeare and vocabulary make a natural combination. Possessing one of the largest vocabularies of any English writer, Shakespeare provides a rich source of the words we need today for improved reading comprehension, effective writing and speaking, and higher scores on standardized examinations. Unlike other books that gloss Shakespeare's words that are now unfamiliar or have since changed their meaning since the playwright's time, this book focuses on words that will increase our vocabulary for current use.

Each of the nine plays introduces 30 key words that are reinforced with exercises and appear in a synopsis of the play. Chapter ten lists the 270 key words from the previous chapters, as well as approximately 1000 additional words from these plays that appear on standardized examinations. Because each chapter is independent, the plays may be studied in any order. Words in boldface appear in the definitions and in the summaries in the same order. *Vocabulary Power Through Shakespeare* builds a more powerful vocabulary while introducing the plays through the study of Shakespeare's word choices.

Acknowledgements

I would like to thank Mark Ishee, Robert Johns, and Adam Meyer for their careful critique of the manuscript and for their patience, encouragement, and kindness. Others who have generously helped in various ways are Lean'tin Bracks, L.M. Collins, Paul McRedmond, Neena Nellori, Priyanka Nellori, Tanya Smilansky, and Betty Woomer. I would also like to thank Fisk University for a sabbatical that made the writing of this work possible.

1. Romeo and Juliet

mar
heretic
wean
boisterous
disparage
choleric
enmity
impute
baleful
sallow
chide
rancor
grave
martial
dexterity

perjure
dissembler
adversity
fickle
inundation
pensive
prostrate
distraught
sullen
dirge
meager
penury
inauspicious
privy
scourge

Learn these words from *Romeo and Juliet*: Set I

1. ***mar*** (MAR) v. damage, disfigure, spoil
A small scar marred the beauty of her face. She had a nearly perfect record of all "A's" marred by only one "B."

2. ***heretic*** (HEHR ih tik) n. person who holds opinions, doctrines and beliefs contrary to those of the church; person who does not conform to an official or established attitude, belief, doctrine, or principle
In times past, individuals regarded as heretics by the established religion could be burned to death. No longer do we think it heretical for women to have the same educational and employment opportunities as men. When the members of the local vegetarian association heard their president talk about the virtues of beef, they considered his speech to be heresy (HEHR ih see).

3. ***wean*** (WEEN) v. stop a child or young animal from nursing on mother's milk; free from a habit, activity, or dependence
Did you know that in Shakespeare's play the Nurse weans Juliet at three years old? Is it better to be gradually weaned from smoking or to break the habit by stopping immediately and completely? The young man must be weaned from relying on his parents to take care of his debts if he is ever to become financially independent.

4. ***boisterous*** (BOY stuh rus) adj. rough; rowdy; noisily high-spirited and unrestrained
The mother warned the babysitter that the children were boisterous and difficult to control. A torrent of words, excessive energy, and unpredictable behavior characterize Romeo's boisterous friend Mercutio.

5. ***disparage*** (dih SPAR ij) v. say bad things about; belittle or discredit
Politicians often make disparaging comments about their opponents. Our soccer coach never disparaged the efforts of any of the players; instead, she always encouraged us and made us feel that everyone was important to the team.

6. ***choleric*** (KOL uh rik) adj. hot-tempered, easily angered, irascible
My choleric boss explodes quicker than a lit firecracker; you might say he suffers from choler since he is always "hot under the collar."

2

7. ***enmity*** (EN mih tee) n. hatred; ill will
The film *Eternal Enemies: Lions and Hyenas* shows the savage fighting and bitter enmity between these two species. Enemies feel enmity toward each other.

8. ***impute*** (im PUTE—rhymes with "cute") v. blame or charge with; attribute, ascribe
Are you imputing that I did something wrong? I resent the imputation that I must have cheated on the examination since I could not have done so well on my own. Do not impute your faults to me.

Working With Words

Complete the following sentences by using each of the following words only once: mar, heretic, wean, boisterous, disparage, choleric, enmity, impute.

1. I am timid, shy, and quiet; my brother is rough, rowdy, and
_____.

2. As my mother recovers from stomach surgery, we gradual-
ly_____ her from a diet of thin soup to meals of whole
vegetables, bread, and meat.

3. With the words "with malice toward none, with charity for all,"
Abraham Lincoln stated in his *Second Inaugural Address* that he bore
no _____ to the South.

4. Many people hoped that the undefeated heavyweight champion
would not come out of retirement to fight again and suffer a loss that
would _____ his perfect record.

5. Do not _____ignorance to people from foreign countries just because they cannot speak English well; they may be better
educated than you.

6. Wouldn't it be surprising if we heard a politician praise rather than
_____ his opponent during an election campaign?

7. In times past, a _____who professed beliefs different
than the religious authorities could be burned to death.

8. I was warned not to say anything that would provoke my hot-tempered, _____ uncle.

Match the word on the left with its definition.

___1. choleric   a. damage, spoil
___2. impute   b. hot-tempered
___3. boisterous   c. rough, rowdy, unrestrained
___4. mar   d. free from dependence on
___5. heretic   e. blame or charge with; attribute
___6. wean   f. person who does not conform to an
___7. disparage   established belief
___8. enmity   g. say bad things about; belittle,
                           discredit
                    h. hatred

Words in context of *Romeo and Juliet*

Romance, passion, feverish first love. For over four hundred years *Romeo and Juliet* has been the quintessential representation of young love in its purest innocence and most passionate intensity. Romeo and Juliet's first glimpse of each other ignites an attraction so powerful that it swiftly surmounts the barrier of fierce hatred between their two families. Tragically, however, the deadly enmity between their families will make their union short-lived. Romeo and Juliet are "a pair of star-crossed lovers." In a period that believed in astrology—the power of the stars and planets to influence or determine a person's fate—the young couple are destined for disaster. It will take the death of these two innocent lovers to extinguish the hatred that has made their families mortal enemies.

As the play opens, servants of Capulet (Juliet's family) quarrel with servants of Montague (Romeo's family). Romeo's friend and cousin Benvolio comes upon the scene and takes out his sword in an attempt to restore peace. Tybalt, Juliet's cousin, then appears and sees Benvolio with his drawn sword. When the latter explains that he is trying to stop the fighting, Tybalt refuses to accept his explanation:

> What! Drawn, and talk of peace? I hate the word
> As I hate hell, all Montagues, and thee.

Clearly, the fiery Tybalt yearns for a fight. As he attacks Benvolio, the brawl escalates, attracting the parents of both Romeo and Juliet to the battle. The Prince of Verona (a city in Italy where the action takes place) then comes with his troops to quell the fighting. The prince warns old Capulet and Montague that this is the third time their family feud has endangered the city of Verona and that the next time they break the peace the penalty will be death.

After everyone disperses except for Benvolio, Romeo appears. Benvolio then asks why his cousin is sad. Romeo replies that a girl he loves does not love him in return. He then notices signs of the recent scuffle and proceeds to bombard Benvolio with a torrent of words about love and hate:

> Here's much to do with hate, but more with love;
> Why then, O brawling love! O loving hate!
> O anything of nothing first create.

> O heavy lightness, serious vanity,
> Misshapen chaos of well-seeming forms,
> Feather of lead, bright smoke, cold fire, sick health,
> Still-waking sleep, that is not what it is!
> This love feel I, that feel no love in this.
> Dost thou not laugh?

If this speech seems like nonsense, for the most part it is. It certainly strikes Benvolio as humorous as we deduce his response from Romeo's last sentence, "Dost thou not laugh?" Romeo has employed figures of speech composed of seeming contradictions such as "heavy lightness," "cold fire" and "sick health" in his commentary about love and hate. These figures of speech, known as "oxymorons," suggest Romeo's immaturity regarding love—a cleverness and egoism devoid of any true knowledge.

Love, or more specifically marriage, is also the concern of Paris, a young count and kinsman to the Prince. Capulet responds to Paris's suit for Juliet by saying,

> My child is yet a stranger in the world,
> She hath not seen the change of fourteen years;
> Let two more summers wither in their pride
> Ere [before] we may think her ripe to be a bride.

Paris counters,

> Younger than she are happy mothers made.

To which Capulet replies,

> And too soon **marred** are those so early made.
> Earth hath swallowed all my hopes but she;
> She is the hopeful lady of my earth.
> But woo her, gentle Paris, get her heart,
> My will to her consent is but a part.

A good father, Capulet is not ready to give his daughter, who is not yet fourteen, in marriage to Count Paris, a tempting prospect since he is kin to Verona's ruling prince. Paris's rejoinder makes us aware that thirteen-year-old mothers were not considered an anomaly during this time period. Protectively, Capulet adds that these young mothers are too soon **marred** or ruined. His concern for Juliet is readily understandable as we learn that she is his only surviving child. However, thinking that a union with a powerful family will most likely insure his daughter's well-being and probably also his own, Capulet adds that he will consent to the early marriage if Paris wins Juliet's heart.

On a less serious note, we find Romeo pining for his unattainable love Rosaline as an illiterate Capulet servant, sent with a message to request certain persons to a Capulet party that evening, asks him to read aloud the names on the list. After the servant leaves, Romeo's companion Benvolio suggests that they crash the party with the intention that Verona's beauties will distract Romeo from Rosaline, who, by the way, will also be there. Romeo swears that he will be constant to his love:

> When the devout religion of mine eye
> Maintains such falsehood, then turn tears to fire,
> And these who, often drowned, could never die,
> Transparent **heretics**, be burnt for liars!

Romeo's ornate statement essentially means that if his eyes are untrue to Rosaline by seeing anyone else as more beautiful, then his eyes should be burnt as **heretics**. In other words, since Rosaline is the true religion of his eye, any turning from her to another woman will brand his eyes as **heretics** or false believers who have strayed from the true faith. As, unfortunately, men and women who departed from the true religion as defined by those in power were actually put to the stake and set on fire during this period, so will Romeo's eyes be burnt. Once again, as with his oxymorons of loving-hate, Romeo's linguistic embellishments—which juxtapose a serious charring of flesh with a fantastical burning of eyeballs to highlight the discrepancy between authentic love and Romeo's soppy state—serve not to dignify his emotion but to trivialize it.

Meanwhile, Lady Capulet approaches her daughter Juliet with the prospect of marriage. In this scene, we learn Juliet's exact age and become cognizant of Renaissance nursing practices through Shakespeare's lusty comic creation—Juliet's nurse. After Juliet's mother says that it is a "fortnight" (two weeks) and a few days until Lammas, a former English church harvest festival celebrated on August 1, the nurse says about Juliet,

> Come Lammas Eve at night shall she be fourteen.
> Susan and she—God rest all Christian souls!—
> Were of an age. Well, Susan is with God;
> She was too good for me....
> 'Tis since the earthquake now eleven years;
> And she was **weaned**—I never shall forget it—
> Of all the days of the year, upon that day.

The nurse establishes that in a little more than two weeks, the thirteen-year-old Juliet will have her next birthday. But the nurse reveals more. The nurse's daughter Susan was the same age as Juliet, but soon after birth died and thus "is with God." It was common practice at this time for an upper-class mother to hire some lactating woman from a lower class to be a nurse. The nurse has thus literally nursed Juliet from infancy and been her constant companion and confidant since birth.

Luxuriating in physical detail, the nurse goes on to describe how she **weaned** or stopped Juliet from nursing by means of smearing a bitter herbal preparation on her breasts. Because this event happened "since the earthquake now eleven years" (i.e., eleven years ago) and Juliet will soon be fourteen, evidently it was not uncommon to breastfeed a child until three years old. The nurse, however, is merely warming to her descriptive task. She then recounts how her deceased husband picked up the three-year-old Juliet after she bumped her forehead by falling and joked,

> Dost thou fall upon thy face?
> Thou wilt fall backward when thou has more wit Juliet,

to which Juliet unknowingly answered "ay" (yes). The implication was that when little Juliet grew up, instead of stumbling forward she would fall backward to receive a lover. Now, says the nurse, the jest has obviously come true since Lady Capulet is broaching the subject of marriage. Delighted with the jest, the nurse repeats it for sheer joy. The nurse's account not only fixes Juliet's exact age and describes **weaning** practices during the Renaissance, but also portrays the earthy nature of the nurse who displays no squeamishness; on the contrary, the nurse exuberantly exults in her narration of the facts of life. The scene ends with Lady Capulet corroborating Paris's earlier statement about the youthfulness of upper-class brides as she tells Juliet about Paris's marriage proposal,

Well, think of marriage now. Younger than you,
Here in Verona, ladies of esteem,
Are made already mothers. By my count,
I was your mother much upon these years that you are now a maid.

Incidentally, Lady Capulet discloses her own age as approximately twenty-eight when she says that she was about Juliet's age when she herself became a mother.

Meanwhile, Romeo, Benvolio and another good friend Mercutio make ready for Capulet's party. Names can be suggestive in Shakespeare as in the case of Romeo's two friends. Benvolio's name is derived from the Latin word part *bene* meaning "well, good" and *vol* meaning "wish, will"; indeed, Benevolio is "benevolent" ("kind, well-meaning"), a word derived from these word parts. Benevolio does wish people well, as evidenced earlier by his attempting to separate the feuding Montague and Capulet servants. Mercutio, too, is aptly named for he recalls the Roman god Mercury, messenger of the gods and known for his slyness and craft—also the protector of thieves and liars. Our word "mercurial" meaning "changeable, unpredictable, lively" stems from this source. Volatile and unpredictable Mercutio certainly is, as well as a verbal fabricator in love with his own words. On the way to Capulet's party, Mercutio teases Romeo about love. Romeo responds that love "is too rough, / Too rude, too **boisterous**; and it pricks like a thorn." Mercutio, not Romeo, is the one who is too **boisterous** because he is rough, rowdy, noisily high-spirited and unrestrained.

As we observe Capulet's party, Shakespeare cues us again about a character's age. Juliet's father asks a relative how long has it been since they were at a masque (a theatrical entertainment with music and dance performed by masked actors). The relative answers that it was at the wedding of someone whose son is now thirty. Since it is reasonable to assume that Capulet probably attended these masques until his late twenties, one surmises that he must be around sixty years old.

When Romeo enters the party, he sees Juliet and exclaims,

O, she doth teach the torches to burn bright!...
Did my heart love till now? Forswear it, sight!
For I ne'er saw true beauty till this night.

Love, however, is not on Tybalt's mind. He recognizes Romeo (even though this is a masked party and Romeo's face is hidden) and vehemently informs Capulet. Juliet's father tells Tybalt to take it easy:

> Content thee, gentle coz, let him alone;
> 'A bears him like a portly [dignified, well-behaved] gentleman.
> And, to say truth, Verona brags of him
> To be a virtuous and well-governed youth.
> I would not for the wealth of all this town
> Here in my house do him **disparagement**.

As befits his years, Capulet counsels Tybalt to accept the situation calmly and not **disparage** or say bad things about Romeo, informing us that Romeo must be a decent youth if he can be praised by his family's enemy. The fiery Tybalt, however, will not be calmed. He exclaims, "I'll not endure him." Now it is Capulet's turn to explode:

> He shall be endured.
> What, goodman boy! I say he shall. Go to!
> Am I the master here, or you? Go to!
> You'll make a mutiny among my guests.
> You will set cock-a-hoop [cause chaos]! you'll be the man!

With the full force of his three-score years—age was respected and a sign of authority in Shakespeare's time—the Capulet patriarch puts down Tybalt. To refer to an adult as "boy" during the Elizabethan period was an insult, a term of disrespect like the **disparaging** use of "boy" when directed by a person of European descent to a mature male African American. Tybalt submits to Capulet, but with difficulty:

> Patience perforce with willful **choler** meeting
> Makes my flesh tremble in their different greeting.
> I will withdraw; but this intrusion shall
> Now seeming sweet convert to bitterest gall.

Forced ("perforce") patience mixes with Tybalt's feelings of **choler** or anger. The **choleric** or hot-tempered Tybalt reluctantly leaves the room but takes his anger with him.

At this point, Romeo meets Juliet, speaks with her, and concludes by kissing his newfound love—all within the space of fourteen lines. In fact,

11

their initial encounter consists of a dialogue that is actually a sonnet or poem of fourteen lines. Juliet then briefly goes to her mother. During this time the Nurse informs Romeo that Juliet is Capulet's daughter. Romeo then prepares to leave with his friends as Juliet returns to the nurse. Juliet, like Romeo, has fallen in love at first sight. However, she camouflages her passion as she tries to find out Romeo's identity:

> **Juliet**: Come hither, Nurse. What is yond gentleman?
> **Nurse**: The son and heir of old Tiberio.
> **Juliet**: What's he, that now is going out of door?
> **Nurse**: Marry [a mild oath meaning "by the Virgin Mary"],
>   that I think is young Petruchio.
> **Juliet**: What's he, that follows there, that would not dance?
> **Nurse**: I know not.
> **Juliet**: Go, ask his name.—If he be married,
>   My grave is like to be my wedding-bed.
> **Nurse**: His name is Romeo, and a Montague;
>   The only son of your great enemy.

So as not to arouse suspicion about her true feelings, Juliet first asks about two men she cares nothing about. When the nurse returns with the information that Romeo is a Montague, Juliet exclaims, "My only love sprung from my only hate!" The tragedy of the "star-crossed lovers" has been set in motion.

After leaving the party, Romeo hides outside Capulet's orchard as he hears his friends Benvolio and Mercurtio approach. Still thinking that Romeo is in love with Rosaline, Mercutio light-heartedly makes fun of Romeo's infatuation. As the friends leave, Romeo comments,

> He jests at scars that never felt a wound.

Romeo scales the walls of the orchard, sees Juliet at her window, and exclaims,

> But, soft! What light through yonder window breaks?
> It is the east, and Juliet is the sun!

Juliet then comes out on the balcony and, unaware of Romeo's presence, declares her love,

O Romeo, Romeo, wherefore art thou Romeo?
Deny thy father, and refuse thy name;
Or, if thou wilt not, be but sworn my love,
And I'll no longer be a Capulet....
What's in a name? That which we call a rose
  By any other name would smell as sweet.

Romeo then reveals himself. Startled, Juliet tells him to leave immediately before her kinsmen kill him. Gallantly, Romeo replies,

Alack, there lies more peril in thine eye
Than twenty of their swords! Look thou but sweet,
And I am proof [armored] against their **enmity**.

If Juliet looks on him favorably, Romeo declares that will be enough to protect him against the deadly **enmity** or hatred of her family. Juliet then emphasizes the seriousness of her love which she so openly declared when she thought she was alone:

                    Therefore pardon me,
And not **impute** this yielding to light love,
Which the dark night hath so discovered.

She tells Romeo not to **impute** or judge her love trivial just because it was so honestly and directly stated. If his intent is marriage, Juliet says he should inform her by a messenger she will send him tomorrow. After Romeo agrees to meeting the messenger, Juliet ends their meeting:

Good-night, good-night! Parting is such sweet sorrow
That I shall say good-night till it be morrow.

Learn these words from *Romeo and Juliet.* Set II

1. *baleful* (BAYL ful) adj. harmful, evil, deadly
Beware the baleful bites of black widow spiders, venomous snakes, and scorpions. In supernatural horror tales, baleful omens often foretell some catastrophe.

2. *sallow* (SAL oh) adj. sickly yellow
Because he was underweight, nervous, and of sallow complexion, we suspected that the prisoner had been mistreated. The doctor said that overwork, poor nutrition, and lack of exercise accounted for the patient's sallow appearance.

3. *chide* (CHIDE—rhymes with "hide") v. scold, rebuke, reproach, reprimand
The mother chided her son for eating with his fingers rather than with a knife and fork; she chidingly told him that he would be embarrassed in public. Whereas my mother would nag and chide to correct my behavior, my silent father would rely on his hand and belt.

4. *rancor* (RANG kur) n. bitter hatred or ill will
At the beginning of *Romeo and Juliet* we are told that the Montagues and Capulets hate each other, but we never learn the origin or cause of their rancor. Tragically, it takes the deaths of their children Romeo and Juliet to end this rancor.

5. *grave* (GRAVE) adj. serious, somber, solemn
The unemployed father gravely told his children that they would not receive what they wanted for Christmas and that they could not eat out anymore; metaphorically speaking, he gravely informed them that their life would no longer be filled with gravy. Are we aware of the gravity of the situation as we consume natural resources that cannot be replenished? Medical authorities say that our health will improve if we learn to relax and enjoy life rather than regard every situation as serious and grave.

6. *martial* (MAR shul) adj. warlike, military, pertaining to the armed forces
The two unfriendly nations engaged in martial activities by sending troops to the border. The word "martial" comes from Mars, the Roman

14

god of war. Because of its reddish appearance, the planet Mars was named after the bloody god of war.

7. *dexterity* (dek STER ih tee) n. skill with the hands, body, or mind
Pianists are known for dexterity of hand, acrobats for dexterity of body, and mathematicians for dexterity of mind. The dexterous performer astounded us with her card tricks.

8. *perjure* (PUR jur) v. lie while under an oath to tell the truth
The witness lied or perjured himself to protect his friend; the suspicious prosecuting attorney suspected the false testimony and through careful cross-examination proved the witness guilty of perjury.

9. *dissembler* (dih SEM blur) n. one who conceals or disguises one's real feelings, motives, or thoughts
Don't dissemble, tell me the truth. Every time Pinocchio dissembled, his nose grew longer. A good poker player can bluff or dissemble and not be detected. Hypocrites are dissemblers.

10. *adversity* (ad VUR sih tee) n. misfortune, hard times, great hardship, trouble
Francis Bacon—an English philosopher, statesman, and contemporary of Shakespeare—said, "Prosperity doth best discover vice, but adversity doth best discover virtue." This statement means that in prosperous times we have the luxury to indulge in immoral habits whereas in times of hardship we must constrain ourselves to acting decently and modestly. Some workers suffer under adverse conditions of long hours, low pay, and unhealthy or dangerous surroundings.

11. *fickle* (FIK ul) adj. inconstant, changeable
The "fickle finger of fate" refers to how chancy, changeable, and unpredictable we feel the touch of fortune in our lives. We praise fidelity but disparage fickleness.

Working With Words

Complete the following sentences by using each of the following words only once: baleful, sallow, chide, rancor, grave, martial, dexterity, perjure, dissembler, adversity, fickle.

1. I don't want to marry a _____ lover; I want a faithful partner.

2. My parents constantly _____ me about not doing homework and scold me about not helping to clean the house.

3. Some comedians are hilarious on stage but _____ and serious when not performing.

4. The judge warned the defendant that to _____oneself or lie under oath in the courtroom is a crime.

5. The hero of the novel was generous in times of good fortune and uncomplaining in times of _____.

6. The brain surgeon was renowned for the _____ of his hands.

7. In Shakespeare's *Othello*, the villain Iago is a great _____ who manipulates people by concealing his real motives and feelings.

8. *Romeo and Juliet* portrays the _____ that exits between two families that are deadly enemies.

9. Judo, karate, and kung-fu are considered _____ or fighting arts.

10. The skinny students with their _____ complexions made us suspect that the boarding school was neglecting the health of the residents.

11. Merlin, a wise and good wizard, tried to protect King Arthur against the _____ magic of evil sorcerers.

Match the word on the left with its definition.

___1. dissembler
___2. adversity
___3. chide
___4. baleful
___5. rancor
___6. fickle
___7. perjure
___8. grave
___9. dexterity
___10. martial
___11. sallow

a. skill
b. serious, solemn, somber
c. inconstant, changeable
d. sickly yellow
e. warlike
f. lie while under an oath to tell the
   truth
g. scold, rebuke, reproach
h. misfortune, great hardship
i. one who disguises one's real feelings
   or thoughts
j. hatred
k. harmful

Words in context of *Romeo and Juliet*

R omeo asks Friar Laurence—a hermit, clergyman, friend, and counselor to Romeo—to perform a marriage ceremony. We first meet the friar as he fills his basket with "**baleful** weeds and precious-juiced flowers." The **baleful**, harmful, or deadly weeds and sweet, healing precious-juiced flowers cause the friar to meditate on how plants and herbs can be used for good or evil. He muses that rightly applied even a poisonous plant can have medicinal power and wrongly applied a seemingly beneficial herb or flower can be harmful. When Romeo asks his help in marrying Juliet, at first the friar is shocked by Romeo's new love interest:

> Holy Saint Francis, what a change is here!...
> What a deal of brine [i.e., salt water or tears]
> Hath washed thy **sallow** cheeks for Rosaline.

He reminds Romeo how often his **sallow** or sickly yellow cheeks were drenched in tears for his former love. In defense, Romeo says that Friar Lawrence often **chided** or scolded him for loving Rosaline. The Friar says that this was not love but doting or infatuation. Romeo states that the current situation is different:

> I pray thee, **chide** me not. Her I love now
> Doth grace for grace and love for love allow.
> The other did not so.

In other words, this is the real thing for they both love each other. Friar Laurence still has his doubts, but sees that a marriage between Romeo and Juliet can bring about good:

> For this alliance may so happy prove,
> To turn your households' **rancor** to pure love.

Hopefully, this marriage may dissolve the **rancor** or bitter hatred and ill will between the Montagues and Capulets. Just as Friar Laurence mused that sometimes poisonous plants can be put to beneficial medicinal use, so now he speculates hopefully that a marriage that might under other circumstances be considered hasty or rash can heal a long, **rancorous** feud.

Romeo then goes off to join his friends Benvolio and Mercutio. They are soon approached by Juliet's messenger, the nurse. After jesting with and taunting her, Mercutio finally leaves with Benvolio. The nurse then delivers Juliet's message to Romeo. He agrees to meet her at Friar Laurence's cell to be married that afternoon. The nurse returns home, teasingly holding back Romeo's answer from the frantically impatient Juliet until finally delivering the message. That afternoon, Friar Laurence marries Romeo and Juliet.

Meanwhile, Mercutio and Benvolio chat together as Tybalt approaches them. Tybalt, still resentful of Romeo's uninvited presence at the Capulet party, tries to find out Romeo's whereabouts so he can challenge him to a duel. Mercutio gives no useful information; on the contrary, he tries to provoke a fight with Tybalt. At this point, Romeo enters after having just been married. Tybalt insults Romeo who, to everyone's surprise, takes no offense but replies politely and amiably. Mercutio, unaware that Romeo's behavior is motivated by his recent marriage to Juliet, interprets Romeo's friendly politeness as cringing cowardice. Infuriated, Mercutio provokes a duel with Tybalt. Romeo, still in a conciliatory spirit because of his wedding, steps between them to try to stop the fighting. During this process Tybalt manages to thrust his sword under Romeo's arm and fatally wound Mercutio. Even when confronted with his own imminent death, Mercutio cannot refrain from wordplay. In answer to Romeo's remark about the wound, Mercutio replies with bitter wit:

> No, 'tis not so deep as a well, nor so wide as a church door;
> but 'tis enough, 'twill serve. Ask for me tomorrow, and you
> shall find me a **grave** man....A plague o' both your houses!

By tomorrow, the habitually exuberant Mercutio will indeed be in a **grave** or solemn state since he will be dead and thus fit for the grave. The **gravity** or seriousness of this situation, however, fails to squelch a **grave** pun.

Mercutio's death obliterates Romeo's thoughts of reconciliation between Montagues and Capulets. Enraged, Romeo vengefully draws his sword, challenges Tybalt, and slays him. Uttering the aptly appropriate words, "O, I am Fortune's fool," Romeo flees just before the arrival of the Prince.

Benvolio explains to the Prince how "with a **martial** scorn" Mercutio thrust at Tybalt "whose **dexterity**" answered Mercutio's attack. He then describes how the **martial** or warlike Mercutio was slain under Romeo's arm as the youthful Montague attempted to separate them. Thus, Romeo's intervention rather than Tybalt's **dexterity** or skill accounted for Mercutio's death. The Prince, saddened by the death of his kinsman Mercutio and knowing that he must implement justice, banishes Romeo from Verona:

> Let Romeo hence in haste,
> Else, when he's found, that hour is his last.

The nurse informs Juliet of Tybalt's death and Romeo's banishment, adding a comment on the untrustworthiness of men:

> There's no trust,
> No faith, no honesty in men; all **perjured**,
> All forsworn, all naught, all **dissemblers**.

No doubt, many women at times would concur that men are liars ("**perjure**" means "lie while under oath to tell the truth") and **dissemblers** or concealers and disguisers of their real feelings, motives, or thoughts. Love, however, triumphs over distrust in Juliet. After her first shock and revulsion of Romeo's slaying Tybalt, Juliet quickly comes to her lover's defense. The nurse then relents and comfortingly adds that she will meet Romeo at Friar Laurence's cell to arrange for Romeo to meet Juliet that evening.

In the meantime, Friar Laurence tries to calm the frantically distraught Romeo. In response to Romeo's anguish at the word "banished," the Friar says,

> I'll give thee armor to keep of that word,
> **Adversity's** sweet milk, philosophy,
> To comfort thee, though thou art banished.

The spiritually learned friar believes that philosophy can help sustain us in **adversity** or times of great trouble, hardship, or misfortune. Not Romeo.

> Yet "banished"? Hang up philosophy!
> Unless philosophy can make a Juliet,
> Displant [relocate, transplant] a town, reverse a prince's doom,
> It helps not, it prevails not; talk no more.

In the midst of this chaotic scene, the nurse enters and exclaims that Juliet's condition resembles Romeo's. Eventually, Friar Laurence dissuades Romeo from committing suicide, tells him to visit Juliet that evening, urges him to leave the following morning for the city of Mantua, and assures him that in time others will be reconciled to the marriage so that Romeo will eventually be pardoned by the prince and invited back to Verona.

Having no knowledge of the secret marriage, Capulet—this same eventful Monday—finally agrees to the persistent Count Paris's suit for Juliet and sets the marriage date for three days ahead—Thursday. Unaware of Capulet's arrangements, Romeo and Juliet enjoy a blissful evening as they consummate their marriage. When morning comes, Romeo leaves for Mantua as Juliet exclaims,

> O Fortune, Fortune! All men call thee **fickle**:
> If thou art **fickle**, what dost thou with him
> That is renowned for faith? Be **fickle**, Fortune;
> For then, I hope, thou wilt not keep him long,
> But send him back.

Juliet personifies fortune. She hopes that since fortune is **fickle** or changeable, fortune will tire of keeping Romeo away for a great length of time and free him to return to her.

That same morning—Tuesday—Juliet's parents present her with Paris's marriage proposal. When to his surprise Juliet does not readily agree to this seemingly ideal match, Capulet explodes,

> Hang thee, young baggage! Disobedient wretch!
> I tell thee what, get thee to church o' Thursday,
> Or never after look me in the face.
> Speak not, reply not, do not answer me;
> My fingers itch. Wife, we scarce thought us blessed
> That God had lent us but this only child;
> But now I see this one is one too much,
> And that we have a curse in having her.

With the full force of his age and status, the Capulet partriach gives his ultimatum to Juliet, even threatening to strike Juliet into submission ("my fingers itch"). Of course, it is the heat of anger at having his will defied that makes Capulet say he wishes he had no child and that Juliet is a curse. Likewise, Lady Capulet's angry remark about her daughter—"I would the fool were married to her grave"—is an outburst of momentary vexation. Tragically, their uttered but not truly meant wishes will come true.

As her parents depart and from Juliet's perspective desert her, she asks her confidant since birth—the nurse—for advice. Earthy and practical, the nurse counsels Juliet to forget Romeo and marry Paris:

> I think you are happy in this second match,
> For it excels your first, or if it did not,
> Your first is dead—or 'twere as good he were,
> As living here and you no use of him.

The vulgar though well-meaning coarseness of the nurse reveals itself in the phrase "and you no use of him," implying that Romeo will not be of use sexually (or any other way) because of his banishment. The nurse's remark makes Juliet's isolation complete. The romantically idealistic Juliet utterly rejects the pragmatic advice of her until now constant friend and supporter. When the nurse exits, Juliet reveals the pure passionate intensity and fidelity of her love as she resolves:

> I'll to the friar, to know his remedy:
> If all else fail, myself have power to die.

Learn these words from *Romeo and Juliet*: Set III

1. ***inundation*** (in un DAY shun) n. flood, overflow, overwhelming abundance, deluge
When James Murray (1837-1915), the editor of the *Oxford English Dictionary* (the greatest of all English dictionaries) advertised for volunteers to send him quotations illustrating how words were used in different time periods, he was inundated with replies of many thousands of letters. The inundation of charitable contributions made our campaign an outstanding success. In their senior year in college, students inundate their teachers with requests for recommendations for graduate and professional schools.

2. ***pensive*** (PEN siv) n. thinking deeply in a serious or sad way; thoughtful; reflective
When Edgar Allan Poe's poem "The Raven" begins,

> Once upon a midnight dreary, while I pondered weak and weary,
> Over many a quaint and curious volume of forgotten lore...

the narrator of the poem is evidently in a pensive mood. As Romeo is about to rush off to Juliet, his old friend Friar Laurence advises:

> Wisely and slow, they stumble that run fast.

The old Friar counsels a pensive, thoughtful approach to his young friend who is given to rash actions.

3. ***prostrate*** (PROS trayt) adj. lying or stretched out with face usually to the ground; prone; v. lie flat with face usually downward
The police examined the prostrate body on the cement floor. In the movie *The King and I*, the King of Siam (current day Thailand) expected his subjects to bow down and prostrate themselves before him.

4. ***distraught*** (dis TRAWT) adj. upset, anxious, deeply agitated
The mother became frantic and distraught when the daycare center phoned her to say that her daughter had an accident. Can you imagine how distraught the surgeon was after he realized that he had sewn up his scalpel in the patient?

5. *sullen* (SUL un) adj. gloomily silent, broodingly or resentfully ill-humored, somber, dismal, morose

The actor who played the happy, carefree character was actually moody and sullen in real life. My brother sullenly agreed to do the chores he hated. John's sullenness evaporated when his good friends knocked at the door, presented him with a free ticket, and asked him to go with them to hear his favorite musical group.

6. *dirge* (DURJ) n. a song or poem showing grief for the dead; funeral hymn

I refrained from crying at the funeral until the dirge when I broke into tears. As I heard our opponents break out in their victory song after our defeat, I vowed that the next time we met they would sing a dirge.

7. *meager* (MEE gur) adj. poor, inadequate, scanty; lean, thin

The waiter looked with disgust at his meager tip. No one looks eagerly for a job that pays meagerly. We are so used to our modern lifestyles that we find it difficult to comprehend the meagerness of material comforts for people who still live without electricity and indoor plumbing.

8. *penury* (PEN yuh ree) n. extreme poverty, destitution

Some artists whose works today fetch millions at auctions lived in such penury that they often missed meals so that they could save for their art supplies. The rich businessman quipped of the poor scholar, " Studious but penurious."

9. *inauspicious* (in aw SPISH us) adj. not favorable to plans or hopes; unlucky; having bad omens

"Inauspicious" is the negative form of "auspicious" ("favorable, promising a good outcome"). Dark clouds, rumbling thunder, and hoards of crows overhead inauspiciously foreshadowed the future terrors of our journey. Orphaned, impoverished, and not knowing a word of English, my grandmother came to the United States at the age of twelve and from this inauspicious background became one of America's wealthiest and most influential business leaders. When in ancient times King Croesus asked an oracle if he should invade Persia, the oracle replied that if he did he would destroy a great empire. Croesus thought the reply auspicious and attacked Persia; the empire he destroyed was his own, thus revealing that the oracle had given Croesus an inauspicious answer.

10. *privy* (PRIV ee) adj. having knowledge of something private or secret; private, secret, hidden, confidential
Few people were privy to the Manhattan Project, the United States' secret enterprise to develop an atomic bomb. Although the master controlled the slave's body, he could not be privy to the slave's thoughts.

11. *scourge* (SKURJ) n. a whip or instrument of severe punishment or great suffering; v. whip, torment, plague
Technology used wisely can be a blessing, unwisely a scourge. In Exodus we read how God scourged the Egyptians with ten plagues before they freed the Israelites.

Working With Words

Complete the following sentences by using each of the following words only once: inundation, pensive, prostrate, distraught, sullen, dirge, meager, penury, inauspicious, privy, scourge.

1. In Charles Dickens' *A Christmas Carol*, everyone cheerfully antici-pates the Christmas holiday except for the gloomy, somber, _____ Ebenezer Scrooge.

2. My best friend is _____ to my secret thoughts and desires.

3. The bubonic plague which destroyed about a fourth of Europe's pop-ulation in the fourteenth century was a terrible _____.

4. The single mother remained cheerful despite the _____ of her tasks: parenting, taking care of her sick father, going to school, and having a full-time job.

5. At a wedding we hear a cheerful song; at a funeral we hear a mourn-ful _____.

6. While the guards banqueted, the famished prisoners ate _____ scraps of food.

7. The dark night filled with the howls of wolves and hoots of owls made us feel that this was an _____ time to begin our journey through the woods.

8. My friend was _____ or deep in thought, trying to decide which job offer to accept.

9. The referee counted to ten over the _____ knockout vic-tim.

10. Growing up in _____, she managed, however, by hard work, intelligence, and luck to become one of the richest people in the world.

11. Joan became _____ when she received a failing grade on her report card but felt relieved when the teacher told her that the grade was a printing error and would be changed to an "A."

Match the word on the left with its definition.

____1. penury

____2. distraught

____3. scourge

____4. sullen

____5. dirge

____6. privy

____7. inauspicious

____8. prostrate

____9. meager

____10. pensive

____11. inundation

a. instrument of severe punishment or great suffering

b. unlucky, unfavorable to plans or hopes

c. lying stretched out on the ground

d. thoughtful, reflective

e. gloomily silent, brooding, somber

f. upset, anxious

g. funeral hymn

h. poor, scanty, thin

i. overwhelming abundance

j. having knowledge of something private or secret

k. extreme poverty

Words in context of *Romeo and Juliet*

Paris has preceded Juliet to Friar Laurence. He explains that Juliet weeps excessively for the death of her cousin Tybalt and that Capulet has hastened their marriage in order "to stop the **inundation** of her tears." A quick marriage will put an end to the **inundation** or flood of her weeping by diverting her to a joyous occasion. At this point, Juliet enters the Friar's cell. Paris tries to make conversation with her, but Juliet asks to speak alone with the Friar. Taking his cue, Friar Laurence says,

> My leisure serves me, **pensive** daughter, now.
> My lord, we must entreat the time alone.

The friar thus asks Paris to leave by saying that the **pensive** or seriously thoughtful Juliet needs private counsel.

Alone with the friar, Juliet says that she longs to die and will commit suicide rather than be false to Romeo. Friar Laurence then comes up with a solution. Drawing upon his knowledge of medicinal herbs, he gives her a potion that will make her appear dead for forty-two hours. He advises her to take the potion the following day, that is Wednesday night. When her family find her the next morning and believe her to be dead, they will take her to the burial chamber of the Capulets. Friar Laurence goes on to explain:

> In the meantime, against [i.e., preparing for the time when]
>   thou shalt awake,
> Shall Romeo by my letters know our drift [plan],
> And hither shall he come; and he and I
> Will watch thy waking, and that very night
> Shall Romeo bear thee hence to Mantua.

Resolved to follow this plan, Juliet returns home and tells her father that she has been instructed

> By holy Laurence to fall **prostrate** here,
> And beg your pardon. Pardon, I beseech you!
> Henceforward I am ever ruled by you.

By falling **prostrate** or stretched out full on the ground before Capulet, Juliet acknowledges full submission to her father's will. Capulet is pleased. So pleased that he moves up the wedding from Thursday to Wednesday—the very next day. Alone that evening in her bedroom, Juliet must suddenly decide if she will now take the potion. Terrifying thoughts plague her. What if the poison doesn't work? What if the friar is trying to poison her so that he will not be dishonored by her marriage? What if she suffocates in the burial chamber? What if upon waking to loathsome smells, shrieks, and sights she becomes "**distraught** [deeply agitat-cd]...with all these hideous fears" and goes mad? Juliet heroically quells her fears, drinks the potion, and falls into a death-like coma.

As morning dawns, the nurse comes and finds Juliet apparently dead. She informs the household. Grief-stricken, Capulet laments that festive hymns must "to **sullen dirges** change." The music that should have been a joyous celebration will now be a **sullen**, somber **dirge** or funeral hymn.

News of Juliet's death reaches Romeo in Mantua that same day. Resolved to return to Verona to join Juliet in death, Romeo remembers that there is an apothecary in Mantua,

> **Meager** were his looks,
> Sharp misery had worn him to the bones....
> Noting this **penury**, to myself I said,
> 'And if a man did need a poison now,
> Whose sale is present death in Mantua,
> Here lives a caitiff [miserable] wretch would sell it him.'

Because it is illegal to sell poison in Mantua , Romeo seeks an apothecary whose **meager** or scantily thin looks signify **penury** or extreme poverty. When the poor apothecary hesitates to risk his life by selling a lethal drug, Romeo says,

> Art thou so bare, and full of wretchedness,
> And fearest to die? Famine is in thy cheeks,
> Need and oppression starveth in thine eyes,
> Contempt and beggary hangs upon thy back;
> The world is not thy friend nor the world's law,
> The world affords no law to make thee rich;
> Then be not poor, but break it, and take this.

This speech reveals Romeo's sensitivity to the apothecary's condition. In the short interim between Romeo's soppy love for Rosaline and his present deathly serious relationship with Juliet, Romeo has matured to where he can express compassion for the unfortunate. Reluctantly the apothecary, compelled by his **penury**, sells the poison.

While Romeo is returning to Verona with the poison he intends to swallow at Juliet's grave, we learn that Friar Laurence's letter to Romeo explaining Juliet's simulated death has not been delivered. The letter's messenger explains that on the way he was quarantined because the town's officials thought he might have been exposed to the plague. He returns the letter to Friar Laurence who now rushes to Juliet's tomb.

Unfortunately, Romeo arrives there before the friar; and before Romeo, Paris. Paris, unaware of Romeo's true relationship with Juliet, attacks Romeo. Romeo tries to avoid the fight, cannot, and kills Paris.

Turning to Juliet, Romeo determines to stay forever with Juliet in the funeral vault:

> O here
> Will I set up my everlasting rest,
> And shake the yoke of **inauspicious** stars
> From this world-wearied flesh.

Inauspicious or unlucky stars remind us that Romeo and Juliet are indeed "star-crossed." Romeo then drinks the poison and dies.

Now Friar Laurence enters the burial chamber just as Juliet awakes. Hearing voices, the friar tries to get Juliet to leave with him. However, Juliet sees Romeo and will not leave. Frightened about being discovered, the friar leaves Juliet and flees from the tomb. Juliet, realizing Romeo's motive for taking the poison, joins her lover in death by snatching Romeo's dagger and stabbing herself.

Soon after, Friar Laurence returns to the tomb accompanied by Juliet's parents, Romeo's father, and the Prince. Friar Laurence explains the sequence of events—the secret marriage, the betrothal of Paris and Juliet, Juliet's feigned death, the messenger's failure to inform Romeo, and Romeo and Juliet's mutual suicide:

> All this I know, and to the marriage
> Her Nurse is **privy;** and, if aught in this
> Miscarried by my fault, let my old life

Be sacrificed, some hour before his time,
Unto the rigour of severest law.

He says the nurse can verify his story since she is **privy** or has knowledge of the marriage. Penitently, the good friar welcomes the death penalty if his well-meaning plans contributed in anyway to the tragedy.

Looking upon the dead lovers, the Prince says,

Capulet! Montague!
See what a **scourge** is laid upon your hate
That heaven finds means to kill your joys with love.

Too late, Capulet and Montague resolve their feud by vowing to build pure golden statues of each other's children. They realize, however, that these golden monuments are nothing compared to the loss of Romeo and Juliet, "poor sacrifices of our enmity." They must suffer a terrible **scourge** or tormenting punishment because their enmity or hatred killed their beloved and loving children:

For never was a story of more woe
Than this of Juliet and her Romeo.

REVIEW EXERCISE

Select the definition closest in meaning.

1. martial   (a) warlike (b) heroic (c) abusive (d) soothing
2. chide   (a) laugh (b) make fun of (c) scold (d) question
3. perjure   (a) wash (b) lie under oath (c) pollute (d) approach
4. mar   (a) celebrate (b) advise (c) improve (d) damage
5. choleric   (a) happy (b) brave (c) angry (d) inventive
6. impute   (a) attribute (b) explain (c) contradict (d) support
7. scourge   (a) reward (b) torment (c) blessing (d) protector
8. privy   (a) unusual (b) exciting (c) confidential (d) painful
9. inauspicious (a) unfavorable (b) precise (c) vague (d) misleading
10. distraught   (a) calm (b) thirsty (c) distressed (d) unlucky
11. wean   (a) eat (b) free from dependence (c) lie (d) destroy
12. disparage   (a) praise (b) prevent (c) isolate (d) belittle
13. enmity   (a) friendship (b) laughter (c) vitality (d) hatred
14. inundation   (a) entrance (b) scarcity (c) overflow (d) foundation
15. adversity   (a) leisure (b) activity (c) luck (d) hardship
16. rancor   (a) love (b) soldier (c) administrator (d) hatred
17. fickle   (a) faithful (b) obsessive (c) changeable (d) stupid
18. penury   (a) wealth (b) poverty (c) stinginess (d) generosity
19. sullen   (a) wise (b) silly (c) gloomy (d) joyful
20. pensive   (a) unsure (b) confident (c) perceptive (d) thoughtful
21. dissembler   (a) employer (b) mechanic (c) supporter (d) hypocrite
22. dexterity   (a) skill (b) playfulness (c) aggressiveness (d) magic
23. grave   (a) amusing (b) serious (c) injured (d) unconcerned
24. dirge   (a) ditch (b) orchestra (c) marriage (d) funeral hymn
25. prostrate   (a) stand up (b) lie down (c) sit erect (d) slouch
26. meager   (a) abundant (b) sharp (c) irritated (d) poor
27. heretic   (a) nonconformist (b) scientist (c) thief (d) laborer
28. boisterous   (a) rowdy (b) humorous (c) intelligent (d) peaceful
29. sallow   (a) sickly yellow (b) pale blue (c) healthy (d) gently
30. baleful   (a) hardworking (b) boring (c) harmful (d) exciting

2. Macbeth

corporal

harbinger

impede

dire

compunction

mettle

husbandry

palpable

equivocate

sacrelegious

amiss

indissoluble

parricide

sundry

jovial

mirth

malevolence

blasphemous

resolute

laudable

appease

avarice

niggardly

raze

pristine

bane

petty

fret

prowess

usurper

Learn these words from *Macbeth*: Set I

1. *corporal* (KOR puh rul) adj. physical, bodily
Whenever my father was explaining how I had misbehaved and uttered that ominous phrase "reason no longer suffices" while grabbing me with one hand and loosening his belt with the other, I knew I was in for corporal punishment. Like "corporal," "corporeal" (kor POR ee ul) also means "of the body." When the British philosopher and economist John Stuart Mill (1806-1873) paid tribute to a famous ancient Greek philosopher by saying, "It is better to be Socrates dissatisfied than a pig satisfied," he asserted that intellectual pleasures were greater than corporeal ones. Incorporeal beings such as ghosts cannot be grasped.

2. *harbinger* (HAR bin jur) n. person or thing that signals what will follow; herald
Leaves that change color are harbingers of autumn.

3. *impede* (im PEED) v. hinder, obstruct, slow down the process of
The determined athlete let nothing impede her rigorous training schedule for the upcoming marathon. Although Moses was "slow of speech and of tongue"—perhaps suggesting that his lack of eloquence was due to a speech impediment—that did not impede his being the harbinger of God's plans to Pharaoh.

4. *dire* (DYR—rhymes with "liar") adj. dreadful, horrible, terrible; urgent or extreme
The hurricane left John in dire circumstances: destruction of his home and business; but the direst loss was of his two children who drowned during the storm.

5. *compunction* (kum PUNGK shun) adj. guilt, regret, remorse, contrition
My compunctious dog puts his tail between his legs and guiltily droops his head when I scold him for wrongdoing; my cat, who has no conscience, never shows compunction.

6. *mettle* (METL—pronounced like the material "metal") n. quality of character, disposition, or temperament; spirit, courage

Although he looked scrawny and weak, he showed his true mettle by tirelessly caring for the sick and finding food for the poor during the dire plague.

7. *husbandry* (HUZ bun dree) n. careful or thrifty management, thrift; ("husbandry" can also mean "farming" as in the phrase "animal husbandry" which refers to raising farm animals)
Our word "husband" comes from the Old Norse word *husbandi* which meant "master of the house" and also contained the meaning "a man who has land and livestock." Since most masters were married, the word "husband" in English came to refer to the male spouse. Because the husband was responsible for managing the house, "husbandry" also kept its meaning of "careful management." And, since most husbands were farmers, "husbandry" also retained its meaning of "managing a farm." Hence, we say that we must "husband" our natural resources (i.e., conserve or manage them carefully and economically) to be available for future generations. Also, "husbandry" still retains its sense of "farming"—hence the two meanings of the word. Shakespeare uses the word to mean "careful management or thrift" in *Hamlet* when Polonius gives this advice to his son Laertes in a famous speech,

> Neither a borrower nor a lender be,
> For loan oft loses both itself and friend,
> And borrowing dulls the edge of **husbandry**.
> This above all, to thine own self be true,
> And it follows as the night the day
> Thou canst not then be false to any man.

8. *palpable* (PAL puh bul) adj. capable of being touched or felt, tangible; plainly seen or obvious
The tension in the room during the final examination was palpable. Incorporeal spirits are impalpable.

9. *equivocate* (ih KWIV uh kayt) v. use language misleadingly to deceive
When the old lawyer fixed me with his stare, I could not equivocate but blurted out the truth. Macbeth gets a false sense of security from the equivocal or ambiguous prophecies of the witches.

10. **sacrilegious** (sak ruh LIJ us) adj. violating what is sacred
"Sacrilegious" derives from Latin "sacrilegium" which referred to a robber of sacred objects from the temples or altars of the ancient Greek and Roman gods. The bombing and burning of churches, synagogues, and mosques are sacrilegious acts. After our hometown hero hit the winning home run for the championship, it would have been a sacrilege to even hint at his defects of character.

11. **amiss** (uh MIS) adv. & adj. out of order; wrongly
Although we thought we had restored the kitchen to order after our catastrophic attempt to bake our first cake, our mother instantly sensed something amiss as she returned from work and entered the kitchen.

Working With Words

Complete the following sentences by using each of the following words only once: corporal, harbinger, impede, dire, compunction, mettle, husbandry, palpable, equivocate, sacrelegious, amiss.

1. When we heard that our uncle had to be rushed to the hospital after suffering a massive stroke, we knew that his condition was
_____.

2. The old soldier said you could always tell the _____ of a man by seeing how he reacts when fired upon.

3. In "The Ant and the Grasshopper" from *Aesop's Fables,* the grasshopper sings all summer and starves in the winter whereas the ant practices _____during the summer to store food for later, thus exemplifying the moral that "it is thrifty to prepare today for the wants of tomorrow."

4. My father did not believe in spanking, paddling, whipping or any other form of _____ punishment.

5. When the groundhog doesn't see its shadow on February 2, the groundhog is a _____of spring weather soon to come; if the groundhog sees its shadow, there will be six more weeks of winter weather.

6. The poet said that words seem as _____ to him as paints to an artist and stone to a sculptor.

7. When King Saul offered David a full suit of armor and a sword to fight Goliath, David said that the battle gear would only
_____ him and opted instead for five stones and a slingshot.

8. Don't _____; give me a straight answer.

9. Because they may have a sense of wronging a fellow member of their group, social animals like chimpanzees are more likely to show
_____ than are solitary animals like weasels.

10. We told the librarian that something is _____ since we found the books not shelved in any order.

11. Because the anthropologist was unfamiliar with the customs of the people he visited, he accidentally broke one of their holiest objects, thus committing a _____ act.

Match the word on the left with its definition.

___1. mettle   a. physical, bodily

___2. impede   b. quality of character

___3. palpable   c. something that signals what will

___4. husbandry   follow

___5. sacrilegious   d. use language misleadingly to deceive

___6. equivocate   e. tangible, capable of being touched

___7. corporal   f. violating what is sacred

___8. dire   g. obstruct

___9. harbinger   h. remorse, guilt

___10. amiss   i. thrift, careful management

___11. compunction   j. terrible

                            k.out of order

Words in context of *Macbeth*

Macbeth depicts the lust for power, the torments of a guilty conscience, and the emptiness that accompanies the fulfilling of misguided desires. The play begins with the ominous chant of three witches:

> **First Witch**: When shall we three meet again
> In thunder, lightning, or in rain?
> **Second Witch**: When the hurlyburly's [fighting] done,
> When the battle's lost and won.
> **Third Witch**: That will be ere the set of sun....
> **All**: Fair is foul, and foul is fair...
> .

The witches refer to the battle where the valiant commanders Macbeth and Banquo defeat forces rebelling against the Scottish King Duncan. The witches will rejoin later that day to meet Macbeth. The cryptic or mysterious and puzzling phrase "fair is foul, and foul is fair" foreshadows the ambiguity of their prophecies to Macbeth and Macbeth's continual dissatisfaction even as his wishes are granted.

Immediately after receiving word of Macbeth and Banquo's victory, King Duncan pronounces the execution of the traitorous Thane of Cawdor ("thane" is a Scottish nobleman just beneath the rank of earl) and grants the title to Macbeth. Meanwhile as Macbeth and Banquo return to the king's camp, they encounter the three witches who greet Macbeth

> **First Witch**: All hail, Macbeth! hail to thee, Thane of Glamis!
> **Second Witch**: All hail, Macbeth! hail to thee, Thane of Cawdor!
> **Third Witch**: All hail, Macbeth! that shalt be king hereafter.

and then Banquo

> **First Witch**: Lesser than Macbeth, and greater.
> **Second Witch**: Not so happy, yet much happier.
> **Third Witch**: Thou shalt get kings, though thou be none.

Astonished, Macbeth—who is the Thane of Glamis but knows nothing yet of Cawdor's treachery or execution—vainly commands the witches to explain further as they mysteriously vanish

Into the air, and what seemed **corporal** melted,
As breath into the wind.

In the midst of Macbeth's perplexity at how the seemingly **corporal** or physical witches could instantaneously dissolve, Duncan's messengers arrive announcing that Macbeth is now Thane of Cawdor.

As Macbeth reflects that the witches' hailing him as Thane of Cawdor has proved to be true, he asks himself,

> ...why do I yield to that suggestion
> Whose horrid image doth unfix my hair
> And make my seated heart knock at my ribs,
> Against the use of nature?

In other words, a horrible mental image makes his hair stand on edge and his heart beat violently. The image of Duncan's murder—temptingly anticipated yet abhorrent to his conscience—terrifies.

Banquo and Macbeth come to Duncan's palace where the king announces that his eldest son Malcolm will be heir to the throne (during this time a Scottish king did not automatically pass his crown to his son but instead named a successor subject to the approval of the Scottish nobles). King Duncan says he will visit Macbeth's castle. Hiding his sinister ambitions, Macbeth replies that he himself will be the **harbinger** or herald of this news to Lady Macbeth so they can prepare to welcome King Duncan.

A letter from Macbeth, preceding Macbeth's arrival, reaches Lady Macbeth. As she reads of the witches' prophecies, Lady Macbeth fears that her husband is "too full o' the milk of human kindness" to take the necessary steps that will hasten his ascension to the throne. She determines to drive away any reservation that **impedes** or hinders Macbeth from seizing power and invokes the forces of evil:

> Come, you spirits
> That tend on mortal thoughts! unsex me here,
> And fill me from the crown to the toe top-full
> Of **direst** cruelty; make thick my blood,
> Stop up the access and passage to remorse,
> That no **compunctious** visitings of nature
> Shake my fell [cruel] purpose.

She will rid herself of any feminine softness of heart ("unsex me here") and fill herself with the **direst** or most terrible cruelty that will be numb to any **compunctious** or guilty pangs of conscience.

Once at home, Macbeth discusses Duncan's murder with his wife and then, alone, ruminates on this regicide or killing of a king. He concludes that Duncan is his kinsman and his king to whom he owes allegiance. Furthermore, Duncan is a guest in his house, the bond between host and guest being sacred since ancient times. Lastly, Duncan is a paragon or perfect example of the virtuous ruler. With these reasons in mind, Macbeth then tells his wife there will be no murder. Lady Macbeth has not steeled herself in vain. She insults his manhood and declares,

> I have given suck, and know
> How tender 'tis to love the babe that milks me:
> I would, while it was smiling in my face,
> Have plucked my nipple from his boneless gums,
> And dashed the brains out, had I so sworn as you
> Have done to this.

Macbeth responds,

> Bring forth men-children only!
> For thy undaunted **mettle** should compose
> Nothing but males.

Swayed by his wife's "undaunted **mettle**" or fearless spirit, Macbeth resolves to murder Duncan.

As Banquo and his son Fleance—two of several guests in Macbeth's castle this fatal night—prepare to go to bed, Banquo tells his son,

> There's **husbandry** in heaven;
> There candles are all out.

The moon has set and no "candles" (i.e. stars) are visible. There is **husbandry** or thrift in heaven since the night is pitch black. On this darkest of nights Macbeth prepares for his dark deed, momentarily halted by an image of the ensuing evil:

> Is this a dagger which I see before me,
> The handle toward my hand? Come, let me clutch thee:

I have thee not, and yet I see thee still.
Art thou not, fatal vision, sensible
To feeling as to sight? Or art thou but
A dagger of the mind, a false creation,
Proceeding from the heat-oppressed brain?
I see thee yet, in form as **palpable**
As this which now I draw.

Macbeth realizes the seemingly **palpable** or touchable dagger is but a product of his feverish imagination, rouses himself from this illusion, and kills King Duncan.

Returning utterly distraught from the assassination to his wife, Macbeth wails that he "shall sleep no more." Lady Macbeth tells him,

> Go, get some water,
> And wash this filthy witness from your hand.

Macbeth is not so easily consoled,

> Will all great Neptune's ocean wash this blood
> Clean from my hand? No, this my hand will rather
> The multitudinous seas incarnadine [redden]
> Making the green one red.

Cooly, Lady Macbeth reiterates,

> A little water clears us of this deed,

a phrase that will come to haunt her as she unravels later in the play.

At this point, Macduff—a nobleman loyal to Duncan—knocks to be admitted to Macbeth's castle. In a rare scene of humor, the Porter wakes from his drunken sleep and admits Macduff. He tells the nobleman that drink provokes three things: a red nose, sleep, and urine. In addition,

> Lechery, sir, it provokes, and unprovokes: provokes the desire,
> but it takes away the performance. Therefore, much drink may
> be said to be an **equivocator** with lechery: it makes him and
> it mars him; it sets him on, and it takes him off; it persuades
> him, and disheartens him; makes him stand to, and not stand

to: in conclusion, **equivocates** him in a sleep, and, giving him
the lie, leaves him.

Drink **equivocates** or deceives in regard to lechery or lust since it pro-
motes the desire but too much drink makes a man incapable of satisfying
the desire.

After the brief comic interlude with the porter, Macduff discovers
Duncan's corpse and announces to Macbeth and the other noblemen this
"most **sacrilegious** murder"—the killing of a king was regarded as a violation of the sacred or divine order. Duncan's two sons, Malcolm and
Donalbain, then enter and the youngest asks, "What is **amiss**?" Macbeth
tells him, "You are," meaning that something is out of order or wrong
with him since he has lost his father. The sons confer with each other and
decide that they must flee to safety, Donalbain to Ireland and Malcolm to
England.

Learn these words from *Macbeth*: Set II

1. *indissoluble* (in dih SOL yuh bul) adj. incapable of being broken, undone, or dissolved; lasting, stable, permanent
At one time the marriage bond was considered almost indissoluble so that divorces were extremely rare.

2. *parricide* (PAR ih side—rhymes with "suicide") n. murderer of one's father, mother, or other close relative; such a murder
"Parricide" refers in general to the murder of any close relative, "patricide" and "matricide" specifically to the murder of one's father and mother, respectively. "Cide" is a suffix meaning "kill" as also in "suicide," "homicide," and "regicide" (killing of a king or queen). Perhaps the most famous parricide (specifically a patricide) in literature occurs in the ancient Greek play *Oedipus Rex* by Sophocles when Oedipus unknowingly kills his father and marries his mother. The Austrian physician and founder of psychoanalysis Sigmund Freud (1856-1939) referred to the parricide Oedipus when he coined the term "Oedipus complex" to describe the subconscious hostility in a male child for his father. Ironically, Sophocles' Oedipus, adopted and raised from infancy by a king and queen whom he believes to be his parents, flees his homeland upon hearing a prophecy that he will kill his father—only to meet and kill a stranger who is his actual biological father, thus committing the fated parricidal act.

3. *sundry* (SUN dree) adj. various, several, diverse, miscellaneous, of different kinds
My son's sundry collection of pets included three bullfrogs, two iguanas, a turtle, three cats, a boa constrictor, several white mice and hamsters, a bulldog, and a tarantula.

4. *jovial* (JO vee ul) adj. full of hearty humor and fun; jolly
"Jovial" derives from Jove, also known as Jupiter, the Roman sky god. The Greeks called this king of the Olympian gods Zeus. Astrologers considered that those born under the sign of the planet Jupiter were of a merry and cheerful disposition, hence the current meaning of "jovial." As Macbeth prepares to murder his associate Banquo, his wife tells him to hide his worries and put on a happy face for his evening banquet: "Be bright and jovial among your guests tonight."

5. ***mirth*** (MURTH—rhymes with "earth") n. gaiety, merriment, jollity, joyfulness, happy fun—especially when these states are accompanied by laughter
At the birth of the king's son and long awaited heir to the throne, the court was filled with mirth.

6. ***malevolence*** (muh LEV uh luns—rhymes with "dunce") n. quality or state of wishing evil or harm to others; maliciousness, ill will
In *Twelfth Night* Shakespeare aptly names Malevolio (from Latin word parts *mal*=bad + *vol*=wish, want)—a cold, humorless spoilsport who becomes the butt of pranks by the fun-loving characters. Some people view the world as a battle between good and evil, benevolent and malevolent forces. Malevolence breeds malevolence unless we break the cycle with understanding, forgiveness, and love.

7. ***blasphemous*** (BLAS fuh mus) adj. strongly, abusively disrespectful of God or sacred things; irreverent, impious
When confronted with the choice to blaspheme God or be hacked to pieces, the martyr chose death. The ancient Greek philosopher Socrates received the death sentence for presumably blasphemous teachings; ironically, his moral and spiritual awareness far surpassed that of his executioners. Most politicians would regard a campaign slogan calling for higher taxes as blasphemy.

8. ***resolute*** (REZ uh loot) adj. having a fixed purpose; determined, firm, resolved, unwavering
The cowboy hero's firm jaw, tightly compressed lips, and steely glance manifested his resolute decision to challenge the villainous outlaw to a gunfight. David resolutely accepted Goliath's challenge, whirled his slingshot, and slew the giant.

9. ***laudable*** (LAWD uh bul) adj. praiseworthy, commendable
Martin Luther King, Jr. lauded Mahatma Gandhi, the father of India's independence. The achievements of these spiritual social leaders are laudable.

Working With Words

Complete the following sentences by using each of the following words only once: indissoluble, parricide, sundry, jovial, mirth, malevolence, blasphemous, resolute, laudable.

1. His plan to end world hunger was noble and _____ but unfortunately impractical.

2. Abraham Lincoln fought the Southern states after they seceded because he believed that the United States was _____.

3. He showers benevolence on his friends but spews _____ on his enemies.

4. Santa Claus is always pictured as jolly and _____.

5. Joan's bookshelves reflected her _____ interests in natural history, sports, literature, gardening, travel, sewing, and astrology.

6. The doctors warned Patrick O'Bese that his great girth was not a matter of _____.

7. The prime minister remained unwaveringly _____ in his decision never to yield even one inch of his country's land in his negotiations with the enemy.

8. The Irish playwright J. M. Synge (1871-1909) treats _____ both comically and melodramatically in *The Playboy of the Western World* where the main character thinks he killed his father in a fight, flees to another village, and confesses his crime to patrons in a bar who are awed and laud patricide.

9. Gore Vidal, a novelist, essayist, and playwright noted for his scathing wit and cynicism, wrote *Live from Golgotha* (1992) about a television crew going back in time to cover Jesus' death—a novel condemned by a priest as genuinely _____.

Macbeth

Match the word on the left with its definition.

____1. mirth   a. permanent, unbreakable

____2. parricide   b. impious, disrespectful of the sacred

____3. laudable   c. murder or murderer of a close relative

____4. resolute   d. praiseworthy

____5. sundry   e. various, diverse

____6. blasphemous   f. determined, firm

____7. indissoluble   g. jolly

____8. malevolence   h. merriment

____9. jovial   i. ill will

Words in context of *Macbeth*

T he nobles now elect Macbeth King of Scotland. Banquo reflects on Macbeth's success and fears Macbeth has played foully. However, when Macbeth invites Banquo to an evening feast, the latter says,

> Let your highness
> Command upon me; to the which my duties
> Are with a most **indissoluble** tie
> Forever knit.

Banquo hides his suspicions of Macbeth's wrongdoing by asserting his **indissoluble** or unbreakable allegiance to Macbeth. After Banquo says that he will have to ride away from the palace in the afternoon but will return for supper, Macbeth tells him that Duncan's sons are settled in England and Ireland where they fabricate lies to hide their **parricide** or murder of their father. As soon as Banquo leaves, Macbeth bitterly reflects that he has gained all in vain for the witches prophesied that not his but Banquo's descendants would be kings. He says to himself,

> There is none but he
> Whose being I do fear

and employs assassins to murder Banquo and his son Fleance.

Just as Macbeth is troubled with fears, so is his wife. Lady Macbeth says to herself,

> Nought's had, all's spent [i.e., lost],
> Where our desire is got without content.
> 'Tis safer to be that which we destroy [i.e., kill]
> Than by destruction [i.e., killing] to dwell in doubtful joy

as Macbeth enters her room. Immediately she becomes the supportive listener to her husband as he tells her,

> Better be with the dead,
> Whom we, to gain our peace, have sent to peace,
> Than on the torture of the mind to lie
> In restless ecstasy [agitation].

Macbeth expresses the same sentiment that she was thinking, but now Lady Macbeth tells him not to worry about what cannot be fixed, shake off worried looks, and "be bright and **jovial** among your guests tonight." To be **jovial** or jolly will not be easy for Macbeth who says, "O full of scorpions is my mind, dear wife." However, his mood somewhat changes as he contemplates the forthcoming murder of Banquo and Fleance.

At the banquet, Macbeth commences in a festive mood and tells his guests to "be large in **mirth**," for at this time Macbeth is unaware that although Banquo was murdered Fleance escaped. Informed that Fleance still lives, Macbeth's own **mirth** or merriment changes to terror. He sees the ghost of Banquo, panics, and destroys everyone's **mirth.** After the party breaks up, we are told that more trouble awaits Macbeth because the **malevolence** or ill will of fortune has not affected the great respect that England's king has for Malcolm, the rightful heir of Scotland. Macduff, too, has gone to England to enlist the king's help to gather an army that will restore Malcolm to the throne.

Macbeth decides to seek guidance from the three witches. As they await Macbeth, the witches boil some hellish brew:

> Double, double, toil and trouble;
> Fire burn and cauldron bubble.

Among the ingredients in this delectable stew are a snake's tongue, frog's toe, lizard's leg, bat's hair, and "liver of **blaspheming** Jew." Unfortunately, in this far less religiously tolerant age than our own, Shakespeare's Christian audience would not have been offended—would even have delighted in—the reference to Jews as impious, profane or **blasphemous** slanderers and offenders of God. Macbeth confronts the witches about his situation. They conjure or summon up three apparitions that tell Macbeth:

> **First Apparition**: Beware Macduff. . . .
> **Second Apparition**: Be bloody bold and **resolute**; laugh to scorn
> The power of man, for none of woman born
> Shall harm Macbeth.
> **Third Apparition**: Macbeth shall never vanquished be until
> Great Birnam Wood to high Dunsinane Hill
> Shall come against him.

Like the initial forecasts of the witches at the beginning of the play, the statements of the last two apparitions fit the category of "fair is foul, and foul is fair." They certainly bolster Macbeth's confidence to continue being bloody, bold, and **resolute** or determined in his tyrannical reign because he believes that no man born of a woman can harm him. Likewise, Macbeth feels that never will the forest of Birnam Wood come to his fortress at Dunsinane Hill. However, what he takes to be fair will reveal itself as foul when the statements of the apparitions will prove to be equivocal.

Acting on the unequivocal warning of the first apparition, Macbeth sends murderers to Macduff's castle. Before they arrive, a messenger warns Lady Macduff of danger. She contemplates,

> Whither should I fly?
> I have done no harm. But I remember now,
> I am in this earthly world, where to do harm
> Is often **laudable**, to do good sometime
> Accounted dangerous folly.

She barely gets out this sad commentary on a world where evil actions are spuriously justified as **laudable** or praiseworthy when the murderers stab her and her son.

Learn these words from *Macbeth*: Set III

1. ***appease*** (uh PEEZ) v. satisfy or calm by giving what is wanted; soothe, pacify, conciliate, placate
The slight snack could not appease his enormous appetite. "Appeasement" is often associated with giving in to demands at the cost of one's principles as when the British Prime Minister Neville Chamberlain, known as the "Great Appeaser," granted the demands of Germany's ruler Adolph Hitler in the Munich Agreement of 1938 in an unsuccessful attempt to avert World War II. Appeasement rarely leads to lasting peace.

2. ***avarice*** (AV uh rus) n. greed for wealth
Plato, the ancient Greek philosopher and student of Socrates, said that poverty does not consist in a decrease of one's possessions but in an increase of one's avarice or greed. In other words, constantly increasing wealth makes one not less but more avaricious (av uh RISH us).

3. ***niggardly*** (NIG urd lee) adj. stingy, miserly
"Niggardly" has nothing to do with racial slurs. Chaucer, the fourteenth-century English poet of *The Canterbury Tales*, used the word to mean a stingy person or miser—long before Columbus set foot in the Americas. W.E.B. DuBois (1868-1963)—sociologist, historian, and cofounder of the NAACP—in his classic work *The Souls of Black Folk* on what it means to be an African American wrote about the impoverished condition of education in the antebellum South: "Sadly did the Old South err in human education, despising the education of the masses, and niggardly in the support of the colleges." After finishing his dinner, the miser left the waitress a niggardly tip of one dime. A somewhat difficult and almost exact synonym for "niggardly" is "parsimonious" (par suh MOH nee us).

4. ***raze*** (RAYZ—rhymes with "blaze") v. completely destroy, tear down to the level of the ground, demolish
The demolition company razed the building so that all that remained was a vacant lot. The warrior chief swore that he would raze every home in the enemy village.

5. ***pristine*** (PRIS teen) adj. pure, unspoiled, uncorrupted; of the earliest time or condition

When life gets complicated, we often fantasize about an imaginary past when life was simple, innocent, and pristine. *Romeo and Juliet* captivates us with its passionate yet pristine love.

6. *bane* (BAYN—rhymes with "sane") n. cause of harm, trouble, ruin, or death; deadly poison
Cats are the bane of mice. Shakespeare's *Antony and Cleopatra* recounts Cleopatra's suicide by placing two venomous snakes—baneful asps—on her arm and breast.

7. *petty* (PET ee) adj. insignificant, unimportant, trivial; narrow-minded
Don't worry over petty details. The petty minds of his unimaginative critics could not comprehend the magnificent vision of the artistic genius.

8. *fret* (FRET) v. worry, irritate, annoy, vex
The theologian Reinhold Niebuhr's prayer—"O God, give us serenity to accept what cannot be changed, courage to change what should be changed, and wisdom to distinguish the one from the other"—tells us not to fret over what we cannot control. Many find adolescence the most fretful time of their lives.

9. *prowess* (PROW us—OW in first syllable as in "owl") n. extraordinary ability or skill; exceptional bravery, especially in battle
Martin Luther King, Jr. was famed for his prowess as an orator. Prowess in battle and poor moral judgment are Macbeth's strength and weakness.

10. *usurper* (you SURP ur) n. one who seizes and holds by force without legal right
In *Richard III*, Shakespeare portrays Richard as a monstrous, baneful usurper who murders his brother, wife, and nephews to become king. In her detective novel *The Daughter of Time,* Josephine Tey disagrees with Shakespeare's portrayal of this king by showing how slanderers concocted the myth that Richard III usurped the throne. James Madison, fourth President of the United States, stated in *The Federalist* that the people lose more freedom "by gradual and silent encroachments of those in power than by violent and sudden usurpations."

Working With Words

Complete the following sentences by using each of the following words only once: appease, avarice, niggardly, raze, pristine, bane, petty, fret, prowess, usurper.

1. The _____ maintained his power by ruthlessly murdering all opposition.

2. The general declared that he would not hesitate to use nuclear weapons to _____ the enemy city by bombing it back to the Stone Age.

3. Environmentalists fought to keep the _____ forest from being razed and converted into a gigantic shopping center.

4. Our local exterminator, Herman Bane, referred to himself as the " _____ of vermin."

5. The phrase "you can't see the forest for the trees" means you only perceive the _____ details but not the essence or overall view.

6. Julius Caesar's _____ inspired loyalty in his troops who would follow him anywhere.

7. If you _____ a bully, he will keep demanding more.

8. In Charles Dickens' *A Christmas Carol*, Ebenezer Scrooge is _____ until visitations from three incorporeal spirits transform him into a generous, charitable soul.

9. In other words, Scrooge changed from a life of _____ to one of philanthropy.

10. If you _____ over every petty problem, you will never enjoy life.

Match the word on the left with its definition.

___1. bane   a. one who seizes power wrongfully
___2. avarice   b. extraordinary ability or skill
___3. usurper   c. worry
___4. fret   d. miserly, stingy
___5. appease   e. cause of harm or death
___6. raze   f. destroy completely
___7. prowess   g. trivial, unimportant
___8. petty   h. soothe, satisfy
___9. pristine   i. pure
___10. niggardly   j. greed

Words in context of *Macbeth*

In England and unaware of his wife's murder, Macduff describes to Malcolm how he will restore him to the Scottish throne. Malcolm, however, fears that Macduff plans

> To offer up a weak, poor, innocent lamb
> T' **appease** an angry god.

Not wanting to be the sacrificial lamb that Macduff offers to **appease** or satisfy Macbeth in order to get back in the tyrant's good graces, Malcolm tests Macduff's loyalty by saying that Scotland will suffer more if he becomes king than it ever did under Macbeth. Malcolm says he has

> A staunchless [insatiable or unquenchable] **avarice** that,
>   were I king,
> I should cut off the nobles for their lands,
> Desire his jewels and this other's house;
> And my more-having would be as a sauce
> To make me hunger more, that I should forge
> Quarrels unjust against the good and loyal,
> Destroying them for wealth.

After this description of his **avarice** or greed, Malcolm continues to list his other abhorrent faults until Macduff can stand it no longer and declares that Malcolm is fit neither to govern nor live.

Macduff's outburst of revulsion assures Malcolm of Macduff's self-less concern for Scotland's good. Malcolm then explains that he had slandered himself to test whether Macduff was secretly working for Macbeth. However, Macduff's joy at discovering the virtue of Scotland's legitimate ruler is short-lived. When a messenger appears with news from Scotland, Macduff tells him to "be not a **niggard** of your speech." In other words, do not be **niggardly** or miserly with dispensing information but tell all. A poignant scene follows as the messenger tells Macduff of his family's slaughter. Macduff then rouses himself from his shocked grief and vows with Malcolm to wreak vengeance on Macbeth.

Before the physical forces led by Malcolm and Macduff reach Macbeth, psychical forces have already penetrated the tyrant's castle fortress. Lady Macbeth, who earlier evoked the powers of evil to numb her to feelings of compunction and reassured her husband after he had killed Duncan that "a little water clears us of this deed," now suffers terribly the pangs of remorse. The court physician hears her saying in her sleepwalk:

> Out, damned spot! Out, I say!...What, will these hands
> ne'er be clean?...All the perfumes of Arabia will not
> sweeten this little hand.

When the doctor tells Macbeth of his wife's troubled mental state, Macbeth asks,

> Canst thou not minister to a mind diseased,
> Pluck from the memory a rooted sorrow,
> **Raze** out the written troubles of the brain,
> And with some sweet oblivious [causing forgetfulness] antidote
> Cleanse the stuffed [burdened] bosom of that perilous stuff
> Which weighs upon the heart?

To which the doctor answers,

> Therein the patient
> Must minister to himself.

The doctor cannot **raze** or obliterate and erase her anguish. Macbeth then asks the doctor to find the disease of his country and "purge it to a sound and **pristine** health." Likewise, the doctor cannot purify the country and restore it to a **pristine** or unspoiled and uncorrupted condition. The sinful reign of the Macbeths, devoid of joy and full of anguish, reaps psychic degeneration. Crime does not pay.

Macbeth attempts to rouse himself by declaring,

> I will not be afraid of death and **bane**
> Till Birnam Forest come to Dunsinane.

He will fear no **bane** or ruin and destruction until the witches' prophecy comes true. However, Macbeth plummets to his emotional nadir when an officer announces the death of Lady Macbeth (later we learn she committed suicide). Macbeth broods,

Tomorrow, and tomorrow, and tomorrow,
Creeps in this **petty** pace from day to day,
To the last syllable of recorded time;
And all our yesterdays have lighted fools
The way to dusty death. Out, out, brief candle!
Life's but a walking shadow, a poor player
That struts and **frets** his hour upon the stage,
And then is heard no more; it is a tale
Told by an idiot, full of sound and fury,
Signifying nothing.

Day in, day out, we **fret** or worry and engage in **petty** or insignificant activities as our meaningless lives play out. A messenger then reports to Macbeth that Birnam Forest moves toward the Dunsinane castle. (Malcolm and Macduff's troops have cut down boughs from Birnam Forest to carry before them in order to camouflage their advance on Macbeth's Dunsinane fortress). Macbeth senses the ambiguity of the witches' prophecies as he begins

To doubt the equivocation of the fiend
That lies like truth.

Macbeth learns the full extent of the witches' deception when he confronts Macduff on the battlefield. Macbeth boasts,

I bear a charmed life, which must not yield
To one of woman born.

Macduff then says that he "was from his mother's womb untimely ripped." Technically, Macduff was not born of woman since he was delivered by cesarean section. His mother was no longer alive (and hence no longer a woman but a corpse) when Macduff was surgically removed from her womb. Macduff then kills and decapitates Macbeth.

Although victorious, Macduff's forces have also suffered losses. The son of the commander of the English army aiding Malcolm and Macduff was slain by Macbeth, but not before the youth had demonstrated his **prowess** or exceptional bravery. The atmosphere of victory prevails as Macduff greets the English and Scottish commanders with the "**usurper's** cursed head." As Macduff waves the head of the **usurper** or unlawful tyrant Macbeth, all hail Malcolm as King of Scotland.

REVIEW EXERCISE

Select the definition closest in meaning.

1. indissoluble   (a) unsolvable   (b) melting   (c) solvable   (d) permanent
2. parricide   (a) pet   (b) murderer of a relative   (c) job   (d) child
3. laudable   (a) happy   (b) insignificant   (c) important   (d) commendable
4. appease   (a) anger   (b) divide equally   (c) pacify   (d) feed
5. petty   (a) cute   (b) important   (c) insignificant   (d) nervous
6. avarice   (a) lust   (b) greed   (c) hunger   (d) hatred
7. palpable   (a) friendly   (b) angry   (c) unclear   (d) tangible
8. mettle   (a) pain   (b) quality of character   (c) disease   (d) noise
9. compunction   (a) alertness   (b) joy   (c) complaint   (d) remorse
10. husbandry   (a) thrift   (b) marriage   (c) health   (d) divorce
11. dire   (a) loving   (b) helpful   (c) understanding   (d) terrible
12. corporal   (a) heavenly   (b) physical   (c) intellectual   (d) dull
13. sacrilegious   (a) violating the sacred   (b) sad   (c) unclear   (d) holy
14. malevolence   (a) kindness   (b) ill will   (c) selfishness   (d) control
15. sundry   (a) similar   (b) hot   (c) various   (d) humid
16. blasphemous   (a) blessed   (b) irreverent   (c) magical   (d) explosive
17. amiss   (a) out of order   (b) correct   (c) exact   (d) heiress
18. niggardly   (a) generous   (b) stingy   (c) slavish   (d) powerful
19. raze   (a) praise   (b) conquer   (c) destroy   (d) admit defeat
20. pristine   (a) snobby   (b) pure   (c) unreliable   (d) firm
21. equivocate   (a) treat equally   (b) cut in two   (c) lie   (d) balance
22. harbinger   (a) manager   (b) sailor   (c) lover of birds   (d) herald
23. impede   (a) hinder   (b) help   (c) explode   (d) destroy
24. fret   (a) worry   (b) sleep   (c) capture   (d) conquer
25. usurper   (a) wrongful taker of power   (b) son   (c) wife   (d) gift
26. prowess   (a) horrible fault   (b) weakness   (c) stinginess   (d) skill
27. bane   (a) helper   (b) respected teacher   (c) trouble   (d) luck
28. jovial   (a) majestic   (b) heavenly   (c) jolly   (d) thoughtful
29. resolute   (a) cowardly   (b) hesitant   (c) determined   (d) wise
30. mirth   (a) miracle   (b) courage   (c) seriousness   (d) gaiety

3. Hamlet

impotent	calumny
sully	pander
circumscribe	whet
beguile	incorporeal
traduce	scruple
wax	exhort
brevity	conjecture
paragon	impetuous
quintessence	remiss
ominous	circumvent
epitaph	sultry
malefactor	dearth
melancholy	infallible
aloof	germane
contumely	felicity

Learn these words from *Hamlet*: Set I

1. ***impotent*** (IM puh tunt) adj. lacking strength or vigor, powerless, ineffective
"Impotent" is merely the negative form of "potent" which means "powerful, effective." Without any potent medicine to cure his patients during the epidemic, the physician felt impotent. In a sexual context, "impotency" is the inability of the male to have intercourse.

2. ***sully*** (SUL ee) v. soil, stain, tarnish, defile
Jealous gossipers and scandal-seeking reporters sought to sully the reputation of the wealthy businessman who entered the political race. They indeed sullied his image; even a saint would have difficulty keeping an unsullied reputation in a political campaign. The polluted air sullied our white uniforms to a dull gray. Cinderella's stepmother and two stepsisters refused to sully their hands with cleaning the house and gave all the hard and dirty work to Cinderella. Although Cinderella's hands and clothes were sullied with grime, her soul remained unsullied or spotless and pure.

3. ***circumscribe*** (SUR kum scribe) v. draw a line around, limit, restrict, confine
After her accident, the Olympic gymnast's activities were severely circumscribed for several weeks; she could not walk for more than five minutes at a time, lift anything over ten pounds, or even sit up and read or watch TV for more than a period of an hour.

4. ***beguile*** (bih GYL—rhymes with "smile") v. deceive, cheat, trick; charm, amuse, divert
"Guile" means "deceit, treachery, cunning"; Shakespeare's crafty villain Iago uses guile to make the newly married Othello insanely jealous of his wife. Similarly, the serpent in the Garden of Eden beguiled Eve into eating the forbidden fruit. However, "beguile" need not necessarily imply deception. "Beguile" can mean to "charm, bewitch" as when we are beguiled by graceful dancers or a beautiful melody. I was captivated by the beguiling innocence of my young cousin. The context will let you know whether the word is innocent or guilty of treachery.

5. ***traduce*** (truh DOOS) v. slander, defame, vilify
His enemies traduced the young priest by spreading the lie that he
seduced a member of his church.

6. ***wax*** (WAX) v. grow, increase, become
The moon waxes or grows larger until it becomes a full moon and then
proceeds to wane or decrease in size. Movie stars wax larger than life.

7. ***brevity*** (BREV ih tee) n. shortness of time or expression; briefness,
conciseness, terseness
The writing teacher stressed brevity by telling us to think of every word
as a dollar and to purchase the best idea at the lowest price. Playing off
Shakespeare's phrase "Brevity is the soul of wit," the twentieth-century
American writer Dorothy Parker coined the advertising slogan, "Brevity
is the soul of lingerie."

8. ***paragon*** (PAR uh gon) n. model of excellence or perfection
Beethoven is a paragon of musical genius, Einstein a paragon of scientific genius, and Shakespeare a paragon of literary genius.

9. ***quintessence*** (kwin TES uns) n. most essential part or quality; perfect
example
The quintessence of good writing is clear communication. Many regard
Abraham Lincoln as the quintessential President.

Working With Words

Complete the following sentences by using each of the following words only once: impotent, sully, circumscribe, beguile, traduce, wax, brevity, paragon, quintessence.

1. When Shakespeare's Macbeth finds out that his hired assassins have failed to kill one of his intended victims, the frustrated and fearful Macbeth describes himself as "cabined, cribbed [caged], confined," meaning that circumstances severely _____ him.

2. The basketball star would not _____, soil, or tarnish his reputation by endorsing products he did not believe in.

3. My father would _____ eloquently about the baseball heroes of his youth.

4. Is it illegal to _____ or slander someone in print?

5. Since we were hungry for lunch, we appreciated the _____ of the noonday sermon.

6. Do not let false advertising _____ you into buying worthless products.

7. I felt as _____ as Robin Hood without his bow and arrows.

8. Our music teacher told us that the _____ of becoming a good performer is practice, practice, practice.

9. When reporters questioned the famous athlete about his drinking, gambling, and sexual escapades, he said that he never claimed to be a _____ of virtue.

Match the word on the left with its definition.

___1. traduce   a. model of perfection
___2. sully   b. grow
___3. brevity   c. powerless
___4. paragon   d. limit, restrict, confine
___5. impotent   e. defile, soil, tarnish
___6. beguile   f. most essential part or quality
___7. circumscribe   g. deceive
___8. quintessence   h. briefness
___9. wax   i. vilify, slander

Words in context of *Hamlet*

Murder, a ghost, revenge. *Hamlet* has all the ingredients of a supernatural mystery. Shakespeare fills this framework with complex, subtly delineated characters. Outstanding among these is Hamlet—perhaps the most richly drawn and fascinating creation in all of world drama.

In the chilling cold at midnight, Hamlet's scholarly friend Horatio joins the soldiers guarding the royal castle of Denmark. As they tell him of an apparition or ghost that they have seen twice before, the ghost appears. Horatio speaks to it, but the ghost disappears. One of the guards then asks Horatio why the country works in feverish haste round the clock, seven days a week, forging armaments and preparing ships for battle. Horatio explains that the recently dead King Hamlet of Denmark—Prince Hamlet's father—was challenged to combat by King Fortinbras of Norway, the winner to possess certain lands that each had wagered. King Hamlet slew King Fortinbras and thus gained the lands staked by the Norwegian king. Now Prince Fortinbras, son of the defeated king, has amassed an army to recover the lands lost by his father. Horatio and the guards speculate that King Hamlet's ghost serves to warn them of this invasion. At this point the ghost appears again briefly, and as it disappears Horatio says that he will inform Prince Hamlet of what they have seen.

Hamlet's uncle Claudius—now the King of Denmark and recently married to Hamlet's mother, Queen Gertrude—tells his court that he has written to young Fortinbras's uncle who is now King of Norway about Fortinbras' purpose. Claudius explains to his court that the Norwegian king is "**impotent** and bedrid," in other words powerless and ailing, and that is why he hasn't kept careful watch over his nephew's ventures. King Claudius's letter will ask the old King of Norway to suppress Fortinbras's plan to regain the lands lost to Hamlet's father.

Claudius then turns his attention to Hamlet and tells the prince that he has mourned sufficiently for his father and must now make an effort to overcome his grief. However, after everyone exits leaving Hamlet alone, the prince speaks his first soliloquy (a speech in which a character is alone and speaks his or her thoughts so that they are revealed to the audience). This speech cleary shows that Hamlet is depressed:

> O that this too too **sullied** flesh would melt,
> Thaw and resolve itself into a dew....

He wishes that his **sullied** or contaminated flesh would melt away—that he would cease to exist. He cites as a cause of his misery his mother's hasty remarriage to his uncle—a man for whom Hamlet has only contempt—less than two months after his father's death. As his meditation ends, his friend Horatio enters and tells him of the ghost. Hamlet agrees to join Horatio and the guards that night to watch for the apparition.

Meanwhile Laertes, son of King Claudius's chief councilor Polonius, says goodbye to his sister Ophelia as he prepares to leave for France. But not before he gives Ophelia, Hamlet's girlfriend, a few words of advice. He tells her that because Prince Hamlet is heir to the throne of Denmark, as regards a wife "therefore must his choice be **circumscribed**." Hamlet cannot be free to marry whom he wants because he is **circumscribed** or restricted by what will be a good match for his country. Therefore, warns Laertes, Ophelia should not lose her heart or virginity to Hamlet. At this point Polonius arrives and gives his fatherly advice to Laertes before the latter departs. When left alone with his daughter, Polonius reinforces his son's concerns for Ophelia by telling her not to believe Hamlet's loving words for they are meant to **beguile** or deceive her so that the prince can satisfy his lust. Polonius commands her no longer to talk with Hamlet. Ophelia dutifully consents.

At about midnight Hamlet joins Horatio and the guards. Trumpets blare and cannons boom. Horatio asks Hamlet what this means. Hamlet explains with disgust that these sounds signal the drunken revelry of King Claudius that "makes us **traduced**" or slandered by other nations. The ghost then appears. It beckons Hamlet to follow it. Horatio and the guards, fearing for Hamlet's life, try to hold him back. Hamlet violently pulls away from them and follows his father's ghost. As his friend departs, Horatio notes how Hamlet "**waxes** desperate with imagination." If anything, Hamlet **waxes** or grows increasingly more desperate as the ghost explains how he died. While King Hamlet took his accustomed afternoon nap, his brother Claudius poured a deadly poison in his ear. The ghost tells Hamlet to avenge his death but to leave his mother alone. As the ghost departs, Hamlet swears vengeance against his uncle. Hamlet returns to Horatio and the guards and makes them swear not to reveal what they have seen this night. He also warns them not to say anything if in the future he will "put an antic disposition on," in other words act crazily. Perhaps Hamlet is permitting himself to behave strangely in order to camouflage his future schemes and/or permitting himself a safety valve for his seething emotions.

Some time afterwards Ophelia reports to her father, Polonius, that Hamlet came to her in hideous disarray, uttered piteous sighs, and stared at her as if he had seen the horrors of hell. Since Ophelia had obeyed her father's command not to talk to Hamlet or answer his letters, Polonius now thinks that Hamlet must have truly loved Ophelia and that Ophelia's avoiding the prince has driven him mad. Eager to rectify what he believes was his original mistaken judgment and advice, Polonius goes to King Claudius and Queen Gertrude to explain Hamlet's madness.

As Polonius meets the royal couple, messengers announce that the King of Norway has made his nephew Fortinbras promise never to take arms against Denmark. The messengers also say that Fortinbras requests safe passage through Denmark on his way to battle Poland. Upon hearing this good news concerning foreign matters, Claudius and Gertrude then listen to Polonius about domestic concerns. After a long-winded preamble ironically including the remark "**brevity** is the soul of wit"—meaning briefness is the essence of intelligence—Polonius ends his tedious introduction and tells the royal couple that the cause of Hamlet's madness is unrequited love for Ophelia. Claudius and Polonius then plan to test this explanation of Hamlet's antic disposition or madness by arranging for Ophelia to meet Hamlet while, unobserved, the king and his chief councilor overhear the young couple.

Meanwhile Hamlet's old school friends Rosencrantz and Guildenstern have been sent for by King Claudius to report to him what they think the cause of Hamlet's odd behavior. On first encountering his old friends in the royal castle, Hamlet tells them that he is gloomy and finds no delight in his fellow man:

> What a piece of work is a man, how noble in reason, how infinite in faculties, in form and moving how express and admirable, in action how like an angel, in apprehension how like a god: the beauty of the world, the **paragon** of animals— and yet, to me, what is this **quintessence** of dust?

In the Renaissance view, the universe was composed of four essences or elements, with a more subtle fifth element, the **quintessence** (from Latin *quinta essentia* or "fifth essence"), pervading the other four. Thus, Hamlet says that he finds no pleasure in his fellow human beings even though they are the **paragon** or model of perfection among animals and the **quintessence** or the most refined and essential being formed from the dust or basic elements of creation. Simply put, he is depressed.

Learn these words from *Hamlet*: Set II

1. ***ominous*** (OM uh nus) adj. threatening; suggestive of future evil
The noun "omen" (OH mun) is a sign of something to come, whether good or bad. "Ominous," however, pertains to only the bad. We canceled our picnic because of the ominous dark clouds. Our boss's pinched lips, furrowed brow, and bloodlessly pale complexion were ominous of the company's disastrous financial condition that he would disclose to us.

2. ***epitaph*** (EP ih taf) n. words, especially those on a tomb, in memory of a dead person
In the *First Folio*, the first published collection of Shakespeare's plays in 1623 (seven years after the author's death), his contemporary and fellow poet and playwright Ben Jonson wrote this epitaph in the preface: "He was not of an age but for all time." The epitaph on Shakespeare's tomb-stone reads:

> Good friend for Jesus' sake forbear,
> To dig the dust enclosed here:
> Blest be the man that spares these stones,
> And cursed be he that moves my bones.

3. ***malefactor*** (MAL uh fak tur) n. evildoer, criminal
On the walls of the post office we often see rewards for the most wanted malefactors. After hearing prophecies from three witches, Shakespeare's Macbeth becomes a malefactor by assassinating the king. In *Hamlet,* Claudius murders his own brother, Hamlet's father; Hamlet learns that his uncle is the malefactor and plots revenge. A crime is a malefaction (mal uh FAK shun).

4. ***melancholy*** (MEL un kol ee) adj. sad, gloomy, depressed; n. sadness, gloom, depression
Hamlet's somber and gloomy meditations appealed to Shakespeare's audience since it was then fashionable to be melancholy. Shakespeare's contemporary, the English scholar Robert Burton (1577-1640), wrote a popular treatise of approximately a thousand pages on sadness and depression, aptly titled *The Anatomy of Melancholy*.

5. *aloof* (uh LOOF) adj. reserved, detached, unconcerned
Most people found the famous scientist cold, distant, and aloof; his few close friends described him as generous, compassionate, and loving.

6. *contumely* (KON too muh lee) n. insulting treatment, contempt, rudeness, insolence
The proud and scornful military officer treated his troops with contumely; no one was surprised when in battle he was "accidentally" shot by one of his own men. Do not confuse "contumely" with contumacious (kon tuh MAY shus) which means "stubbornly disobedient, rebellious." Perhaps a contumacious soldier shot the officer who treated him with contumely.

7. *calumny* (KAL um nee) n. malicious lie, slander
The candidate's husband begged her not to become a political candidate because he knew her opponent was a vicious, unscrupulous campaigner who would sully her honorable reputation with calumny.

8. *pander* (PAN der) v. play up to another's desires and weaknesses
"Pander" derives from a character in the long narrative poem about the Trojan War *Troilus and Cressida* by Chaucer (1340-1400), also the author of *The Canterbury Tales*. Pandarus is Cressida's uncle and arranges for her to meet in his house with the Trojan Prince Troilus to make love. His morally questionable manipulation of the lovers has made his name a synonym for the noun "pimp." However, we use "pander" more commonly as a verb meaning to "cater to one's baser emotions" as when pornographers pander to our lust and disreputable stock brokers pander to our greed.

9. *whet* (WET) v. sharpen a knife or other tool; hence, make keen, eager, or stimulate
When my father whets the carving knife to slice the Thanksgiving turkey, he also whets my appetite.

10. *incorporeal* (in cor POR ee ul) adj. not having material form or substance
"Corporal" and "corporeal" both mean "of the body, physical, material." Hence, corporal punishment refers to physical punishment such as a whipping, and corporeal suffering refers to bodily suffering as when cancer patients in their final stages feel agonizing pain. However, today we use only "incorporeal" to mean "without material form, bodiless." When

Hamlet speaks to his father's ghost in his mother's presence, his mother sees nothing and thinks he talks to the "incorporal air." If Shakespeare were writing today, the air would be "incorporeal." "Incorporal" has become truly "incorporeal," without any physical presence in modern day dictionaries.

Working With Words

Complete the following sentences by using each of the following words only once: ominous, epitaph, malefactor, melancholy, aloof, contumely, calumny, pander, whet, incorporeal.

1. Santa Claus is jolly, not _____.

2. In Shakespeare's *The Merchant of Venice*, a merchant borrows money on the condition that if he fails to repay the loan a pound of his flesh will be cut off from whatever part of his body the lender desires; the merchant fails to repay and during the most famous court scene in theater, the moneylender Shylock begins to _____ his knife as he anticipates carving his victim.

3. In Homer's *Odyssey*, an ancient Greek epic about the hero Odysseus returning home after twenty years from the Trojan War, Odysseus disguises himself as an old beggar when he enters his palace now swarming with freeloading scoundrels who wish him dead. They treat him with _____ until Odysseus reveals himself in his full, glorious potency and slaughters these human vermin.

4. The defendant protested that all the charges against him were lies, slander, and _____.

5. When asked whether he felt life unbearable because he had no visible means of support, the saintly man cheerfully replied that he treasured his contact with _____ beings and pitied the person who had no invisible means of support.

6. Fraudulent peddlers of genealogies _____ to our vanity to have an illustrious family tree.

7. The English poet Lord Byron (1788-1824) made the sexist remark that you cannot "believe a woman or an _____."

8. In Shakespeare's play *Measure for Measure*, premarital intercourse is a crime punishable by death. When her brother is discovered to be a _____ regarding this behavior, the heroine of the play pleads for his life.

9. To be successful, a political candidate must not seem _____ to the voters.

10. On my first day of class a bully stole my lunch, I failed to solve any review problems in math class, and a line drive broke my nose during baseball practice—an _____ beginning.

Vocabulary Power Through Shakespeare

Match the word on the left with its definition.

___1. aloof
___2. contumely
___3. epitaph
___4. incorporeal
___5. ominous
___6. pander
___7. calumny
___8. melancholy
___9. malefactor
___10. whet

a. bodiless
b. threatening
c. reserved, detached, unconcerned
d. insolence, insulting treatment
e. words in memory of a dead person
f. sad
g. criminal
h. sharpen
i. slander
j. exploit other's weaknesses

Words in context of *Hamlet*

Polonius somewhat arouses Hamlet from his glum mood by announcing to the prince and his friends that a company of actors have come to the castle. Hamlet welcomes the troupe and asks one of the actors to give a speech about when the Greeks "lay couched in the **ominous** horse." The **ominous** or threatening horse is the great wooden Trojan horse which concealed Greek warriors until they emerged in the night in a surprise attack that brought them victory in the Trojan War that had begun when the beautiful Greek Helen was abducted by a Trojan prince. When the actor finishes his speech, Hamlet tells Polonius that actors "are the abstract [summary] and brief chronicles of the time. After your death you were better have a bad **epitaph** than their ill report while you live." In other words, actors can harm a reputation worse than a slanderous **epitaph** or memorial inscription. Hamlet then plans for the actors to perform a play the next day that will reenact the murder of his father according to the ghost's account. Hamlet has heard that guilty people observing a scene from a play portraying their crime have "proclaimed their **malefactions**." If the scene startles Claudius, then Hamlet will know that his uncle is a **malefactor** guilty of murder. Only by this means can Hamlet know for sure whether he has seen the real ghost of his father that truly recounted how he was murdered or whether the devil has assumed the shape of his father's apparition in order to trap Hamlet, weakened through **melancholy** or depression, into damnation. As Hamlet says,

> The play's the thing
> Wherein I'll catch the conscience of the king

and thus know the reality of the situation.

As the actors get settled in the castle, King Claudius and Queen Gertrude question Rosencrantz and Guildenstern about Hamlet. The friends say that Hamlet admits to a confused state of mind "but with a crafty madness keeps **aloof**" or reserved when they probe for the reason of his agitation. The king then discusses with Polonius how the latter will arrange for his daughter to meet Hamlet seemingly by chance and be overheard as planned.

Ophelia positions herself so as to be in Hamlet's path as the prince strolls in delivering his most famous soliloquy: "To be or not to be, that is the question...." Hamlet contemplates suicide. He wonders why anyone would continue to bear the painful burdens of life such as the pangs of rejected love, injustice, and "the proud man's **contumely**" or contemptuous insolence when suicide would bring quick relief. He concludes his soliloquy by saying that it is the fear of what unknown tortures may await us in the afterlife that makes us endure our earthly tribulations.

His meditation ended, Hamlet then meets Ophelia while Claudius and Polonius eavesdrop. Hamlet harshly tells her that he no longer loves her, indeed never did, and warns,

> If thou dost marry, I'll give thee this plague for thy dowry: be thou as chaste as ice, as pure as snow, thou shalt not escape **calumny**.

No matter how pure one's life, no one can avoid **calumny** or vicious slander. This conversation convinces Claudius that love is not the cause of Hamlet's mad behavior, that Hamlet is dangerous, and that Hamlet must be removed as a threat by being quickly sent to England. Polonius agrees with the Danish king's course of action but asks for one more chance to discover what ails Hamlet. The chief councilor suggests that Hamlet's mother send for her son and speak plainly with him to find out the cause of his strange behavior. Polonius will once again eavesdrop and report the conversation to the king. If this meeting does not reveal the root of Hamlet's malady, then Polonius will send Hamlet off to England.

Before this mother-son meeting takes place, the performers reenact for the Danish court the murder of Hamlet's father. As the actor playing the murderer pours poison in the sleeping player king's ear, the startled Claudius rises, demands light, and rushes out. Hamlet now believes that the ghost has told the truth.

Polonius tells Hamlet that his mother requests her son to come to her. On the way to his mother, Hamlet passes the king in what seems to be prayer. Unknown to Hamlet, Claudius in a soliloquy has just revealed that he murdered his brother. However, Claudius realizes that he cannot be forgiven his sin because he is unwilling to give up the fruits of his crime: the kingship and Queen Gertrude. Hamlet draws his sword to kill the king and then hesitates. If he kills Claudius in what Hamlet wrongly assumes is a state of true prayer and penitence, then according to the religious doctrine of the time Claudius will go to heaven. Better to kill Claudius when he is drunk, in a rage, engaged in lust, or cursing while gambling so that he has no chance of salvation. That would be true revenge.

Hamlet then enters his mother's chamber while Polonius hides behind the drapery. Hamlet roughly confronts his mother, making her afraid so she cries out for help. Polonius responds with his own scream for help. Instantaneously, Hamlet thrusts his sword through the drapery and discovers that he has killed Polonius. The prince then continues to savagely scold his mother for her relationship with Claudius. He tells her that she exemplifies how "reason **panders** will," how reason **panders** to or caters and plays up to her willful lust. At this point the ghost appears to Hamlet but cannot be perceived by the queen. The ghost tells his son that he has come "to **whet** thy almost blunted purpose." The ghost says that he must **whet** or sharpen Hamlet's sense of revenge against Claudius and also tells his son to stop scolding and start soothing his mother. During Hamlet's conversation with his father's ghost, Queen Gertrude looks with astonishment on what appears to her to be Hamlet talking to "the **incorporal** air" because she detects no physical presence. She now regards Hamlet with motherly concern as she fears he has lost his mind. As the ghost departs, Hamlet and his mother reconcile.

Learn these words words from *Hamlet*: Set III

1. ***scruple*** (SKROO pul) n. doubt or uneasiness as to what is right or proper
"Scruple" comes from Latin *scrupulus*, a small, sharp stone that sometimes would get painfully caught in the Romans' sandals. Today, "scruple" refers not to physical pain but to a twinge of conscience. The handsome, smooth-talking swindler had no scruple about preying on bereaved widows. "Scruple" is often used in its plural form, as when cardsharps have no scruples or moral uneasiness about cheating in poker. Scrupulous people have scruples, but "scrupulous" can also mean "extremely thorough, exact, precise" without any moral or ethical import; Olympic gymnasts and figure skaters display scrupulous adherence to form. Unscrupulous persons have no moral doubt or uneasiness. Shakespeare's Macbeth at first has scruples and hesitates about murdering his king but after accomplishing the heinous deed becomes an unscrupulous tyrant without any moral qualms.

2. ***exhort*** (ig ZORT) v . strongly urge, advise, or caution
As I left for college, the first in my family to do so, my parents exhorted me to study hard. Their exhortation was unnecessary because I knew how they had sacrificed to give me this opportunity and vowed to myself to make them proud.

3. ***conjecture*** (kun JEK chur) n.& v. guess, surmise
That we all die is a certainty; what happens after we die is a conjecture. My cynical friend said that stock market analysts should have on their desks the slogan: "Your conjecture is as good as mine."

4. ***impetuous*** (im PECH oo us) adj. impulsive, rash, hasty
Advice to impetuous lovers eager to wed might be: marry in haste, repent at leisure. A variant of this old adage appears in Shakespeare's *The Taming of the Shrew* which portrays lovers more tempestuous than impetuous. As the bride in this play impatiently waits for her tardy groom on their marriage day, she peevishly says he "wooed in haste, and means to wed at leisure."

5. *remiss* (rih MISS) adj. careless in performing a task or duty; negligent
While in school, I could not fully appreciate my teacher saying that she would feel remiss if she did not point out every error in my compositions. The loving couple felt it remiss to leave each other without a kiss.

6. *circumvent* (sir kum VENT) v. get around, prevent, or avoid, especially by cleverness; outwit, evade, elude
It may be wise sometimes to circumvent difficulties "for fools rush in where angels fear to tread." My mother would tolerate no explanations, excuses, pleading, or other circumventions when we tried to avoid doing our chores. Circumventing the traffic jam by taking an alternate route, we reached our destination on time.

7. *sultry* (SUL tree) adj. oppressively hot and humid, sweltering; passionate, sensual
Summer days in the Deep South—usually thought of as Alabama, Georgia, Louisiana, Mississippi, and South Carolina—can be sultry. "Sultry" describes not only weather but also women who are hotly passionate, sensual, and alluring. The English Romantic poet Lord Byron plays upon both senses of sultry in *Don Juan*:

> What men call gallantry, and gods adultery,
> Is much more common where the climate's sultry.

"Torrid" is another word that applies to a hot climate, but to parching or dry heat rather than the moist heat that is sultry. Like "sultry," "torrid" also has a sexual connotation as when we speak of a torrid relationship that blazes with passion.

8. *dearth* (DURTH—rhymes with "earth") n. scarcity, paucity
At our Thanksgiving feast there was no dearth of food. A dearth of food causes famine; a dearth of knowledge, ignorance; and a dearth of hygienic conditions, disease. An antonym of "dearth" is "plethora" meaning "overabundance, excess." As long as we have access to a plethora of refined, sweet, and fatty foods, there will never be a dearth of fad diets, exercise contraptions, and weight-loss pills.

9. *infallible* (in FAL uh bul) adj. incapable of error, unfailing, sure
"To err is human, to forgive divine" means that human beings are fallible or make mistakes and only God is perfect. The French Emperor Napoleon

(1769-1821) had an aura of infallibility about him until his disastrous winter campaign in Russia where he lost 500,000 of his 600,000 troops by death, capture, or desertion.

10. *germane* (jur MAYN) adj. relevant, pertinent
"Germane" derives from Latin "germanus" meaning "having the same parent"; hence, its modern meaning of "related" in the sense of being appropriate, fitting, relevant. The judge told the lawyer to stick to questions which were germane to the case. I was fond of my professor's amusing digressions even though they were not always germane to the assigned lesson.

11. *felicity* (fih LIS ih tee) n. great happiness, bliss; skill and grace, especially in language or art
Good publicity contributes to a celebrity's felicity. Masters of felicitous prose, Thomas Jefferson and Abraham Lincoln needed no speechwriters.

Working With Words

Complete the following sentences by using each of the following words only once: scruple, exhort, conjecture, impetuous, remiss, circumvent, sultry, dearth, infallible, germane, felicity.

1. She would courageously confront fearful situations rather than trying to _____ them.

2. As I prepared to leave for the university, my mother would quote the words of the American sociologist W.E.B. Du Bois (1868-1963) to _____ me that an education means more than increasing earning power: "The true college will ever have one goal,—not to earn meat, but to know the end and aim of that life which meat nourishes."

3. Because there was no _____ of sweet desserts, we all increased our girth.

4. The zoologist had traveled all over the world from the frigid Arctic to the _____ Tropics.

5. Because I love language, I am in a state of _____ whenever I listen to a felicitous speech.

6. Whenever the weatherman says there will be a fifty percent chance of rain, I feel I am hearing a worthless _____ and not a professional forecast.

7. Pencils have erasers because we are not _____.

8. Revise your essays to eliminate anything not _____ to the main thesis.

9. The saying "haste makes waste" exhorts us not to be _____.

10. My mother scolded me for being _____ when she discovered the mess I left after cooking.

11. Only a person without a _____ could cheat widows and orphans.

Match the word on the left with its definition.

____1. infallible
____2. remiss
____3. felicity
____4. exhort
____5. sultry
____6. germane
____7. impetuous
____8. dearth
____9. circumvent
____10. scruple
____11. conjecture

a. avoid, evade
b. paucity, scarcity
c. surmise, guess
d. incapable of error
e. relevant, pertinent
f. urge
g. bliss
h. impulsive, rash, hasty
i. negligent
j. sweltering, hot and humid
k. twinge or pang of conscience

Words in context of *Hamlet*

Gertrude informs Claudius that Hamlet has killed Polonius. Afraid for his own life, Claudius sends Hamlet accompanied by Rosencrantz and Guildenstern to England. Rosencrantz and Guildenstern bear sealed letters from Claudius to the King of England demanding the immediate death of Hamlet. As Hamlet heads for the ship that will take him to England, he encounters Fortinbras's army marching across Denmark on its way to Poland. Hamlet asks the army captain what is the soldiers' purpose. The captain explains that they go to gain a little patch of worthless ground from Poland. The troops depart and Hamlet soliloquizes on the difference between himself and Fortinbras. The Norwegian prince is a foil or contrast to the Danish prince; Fortinbras exemplifies bold decisiveness as he risks his own and thousands of other lives over a petty piece of dirt while Hamlet, who has so much greater motivation to act to avenge a father's murder, has as yet done nothing. Hamlet muses that it may be some cowardly **scruple** or doubt caused by thinking too deeply that has made him indecisive and unable to take action. Hamlet says that the examples of Fortinbras and his army **exhort** or strongly urge him to take revenge on his uncle. The Prince of Denmark concludes his soliloquy with the remark that from now on his thoughts will be worthless unless they focus on bloody vengeance.

As Hamlet leaves for England, more tragedy strikes the Danish court. Devastated by the death of her father, Ophelia has gone mad. Horatio tells Gertrude to speak to Ophelia, for her insane ravings could cause "dangerous **conjectures**" or guesses among troublemakers. The king and queen talk to Ophelia, but her madness is impenetrable.

Informed of his father's death and assuming Claudius responsible, Laertes with "**impetuous** haste" impulsively speeds home to Denmark. Laertes, like Fortinbras, is a foil to Hamlet for he immediately acts to avenge his father's murder. Laertes breaks down the castle doors, rushes in, and grabs Claudius. Queen Gertrude tells Laertes that the king did not kill Polonius. The crafty king then says that it will clearly be shown that he is guiltless of the deed and also grieves for the loss. At this point the insane Ophelia enters. The agony of this sight intensifies Laertes's desire for vengeance. Claudius assures Laertes he will help him get revenge.

Following this scene, Horatio receives a letter from Hamlet saying that pirates attacked his ship. In the skirmish, Hamlet leaped on the pirate ship and became a prisoner as the other ship continued with Rosencrantz and Guildenstern to England. Hamlet says he was well treated by the pirates and is now returning to Denmark. He tells Horatio he has also sent letters to the king and asks Horatio to meet him when he returns to Denmark. Later we learn that Hamlet discovered the letters carried by Rosencrantz and Guildenstern that commanded the English king to kill Hamlet. Hamlet stealthily replaced these letters with other ones that order the King of England to put the bearers of these letters—Rosencrantz and Guildenstern (who are unaware of the contents of the letters they deliver)—to sudden death.

We then find Claudius explaining how Hamlet meant to kill him as well as Polonius as the king lures Laertes into a plot against the prince. But his conversation with Laertes is interrupted as a messenger delivers Hamlet's letters to Claudius. Reading that Hamlet has returned to Denmark and asks permission to see him tomorrow, the shocked king falters momentarily but quickly regains his composure as he determines to put an end to Hamlet. Claudius then discloses his plot. Laertes will fight in a fencing match with Hamlet. The dual will supposedly be with swords with blunted tips. However, once the match begins, Laertes will select a sword whose tip is sharp, which action will go unnoticed by the **remiss** or negligent Hamlet who suspects no treachery. To make doubly sure of success, Laertes says that he will put poison on the tip of his sword. And just to make the scheme foolproof, Claudius adds that he will prepare a poisoned cup of wine for Hamlet to drink as he works up a thirst during the fencing match. Queen Gertrude enters at this point with the news that Ophelia has drowned.

Hamlet and Horatio then appear at the site where a gravedigger prepares Ophelia's grave. As the gravedigger throws up a skull, Hamlet cynically comments that it might have been the head of a crafty politician who "would **circumvent** God" or cleverly elude the Almighty if given the chance. The gravedigger says that he has been at his job for thirty years since the birth of Prince Hamlet. When Hamlet picks up another skull, the gravedigger says that it belonged to Yorick, the court jester, who died twenty-three years ago. Hamlet reminisces how in his childhood he was carried on the back of Yorick. The graveyard scene thus establishes Hamlet's age at about thirty.

At this point Ophelia's funeral session appears. Hamlet and Horatio watch as Ophelia is laid in the grave. Laertes then leaps into the grave to hold his sister for one final moment. Hamlet reveals himself when he, too, jumps into the grave to say his last farewell to his beloved. Laertes and Hamlet grapple but are quickly parted by Claudius's men.

In the following scene Hamlet receives a challenge from Laertes to what Hamlet believes is a friendly fencing match to reconcile them after their skirmish. Osric, an overcourteous nobleman, delivers the challenge. Hamlet decides to play with this excessively fashionable and courteous member of the royal court. When the courtier says that it is very hot, Hamlet says that it is very cold. The courtier readily agrees. Then Hamlet says that "it is very **sultry** and hot." Once again the courtier reverses his opinion and says that it is exceedingly **sultry** or hot and humid. The court dandy then flatteringly describes Laertes in grandiloquent, excessively inflated language. Hamlet parodies the exaggerated speech of the courtier and agrees that Laertes' qualities are of such "**dearth** and rarity" that no one can even approximate them. Osric politely responds that Hamlet "speaks most **infallibly**" or without any error about Laertes's many excellent qualities of which there is a **dearth** or scarcity in everyone else. Osric then says that King Claudius has bet with Laertes that Hamlet will win the match. Part of the wager includes some very well-made and richly ornamented "carriages," another word for "sword straps." Continuing to poke fun at Osric, Hamlet refers to the word "carriages" and says that the word "would be more **germane** to the matter if we could carry a cannon by our sides." Since cannons are mounted and carried on "carriages," the word "carriage" would be more **germane** or appropriate if one dangled a cannon from the "carriage" (strap) about one's waist rather than a sword.

After this banter, Hamlet and Laertes meet for their duel. Hamlet scores the first hit. Then Claudius offers him the poisoned wine. However, Hamlet forgoes the wine since he is eager to continue the match. He scores a second hit. Queen Gertrude at this point takes the poisoned cup to drink to her son's health. Claudius tries to stop her, but he is too late. Laertes then wounds Hamlet with the poisoned tip of his blade. Surprised and angered by the use of an unblunted rapier, Hamlet scuffles with Laertes. They pick up each other's swords, and Hamlet wounds Laertes with the poisoned blade. Hamlet's mother then screams that she is poisoned. Repentant, the dying Laertes confesses the plot and says the king is to blame. Hamlet stabs Claudius with the poisoned rapier and pours the deadly wine down his uncle's throat. Watching with horrendous sorrow, Horatio then grabs the cup with the intention of swallowing the remaining contents in order to accompany his friend in death. Hamlet, however, wrestles the cup from him. He tells Horatio,

If thou didst ever hold me in thy heart,
Absent thee from **felicity** awhile,

And in this harsh world draw thy breath in pain
To tell my story.

For Hamlet life is pain and death is **felicity** or bliss. He thus asks his dear friend to remain alive in this painful world and forgo awhile the **felicity** of eternal bliss in order to tell Hamlet's tragic story. Hamlet dies as Horatio mournfully says,

Now cracks a noble heart. Good night, sweet prince,
And flights of angels sing thee to thy rest.

REVIEW EXERCISE
Select the definition closest in meaning.

1. aloof   (a) playful (b) athletic (c) detached (d) comforting
2. epitaph   (a) curse (b) tombstone inscription (c) slander (d) enemy
3. scruple   (a) intelligence (b) hate (c) moral uneasiness (d) love
4. sultry   (a) slimy (b) smooth (c) sweltering (d) rough
5. remiss   (a) negligent (b) responsible (c) exact (d) true
6. conjecture   (a) pain (b) pleasure (c) guess (d) sorrow
7. sully   (a) soil (b) drown (c) grow (d) race
8. paragon   (a) perfect example (b) child (c) animal (d) dirt
9. circumscribe (a) confine (b) anger (c) calm (d) stimulate
10. beguile   (a) smile (b) torture (c) deceive (d) help
11. traduce   (a) pray (b) slander (c) praise (d) argue
12. quintessence (a) most essential part (b) weapons (c) magic (d) glory
13. impotent   (a) powerful (b) drunk (c) powerless (d) sober
14. calumny   (a) malicious lie (b) poetry (c) sin (d) stupidity
15. pander   (a) cater to low desires (b) success (c) stop (d) spoil
16. malefactor   (a) blessing (b) disease (c) criminal (d) reward
17. whet   (a) drown (b) conquer (c) cry (d) sharpen
18. circumvent   (a) surround (b) evade (c) avoid (d) show off
19. impetuous   (a) impulsive (b) repulsive (c) dull (d) irritating
20. germane   (a) foreign (b) relevant (c) pleasant (d) painful
21. brevity   (a) undergarments (b) forest (c) joy (d) briefness
22. ominous   (a) threatening (b) generous (c) supportive (d) angry
23. wax   (a) shrink (b) perspire (c) neglect (d) grow
24. incorporeal   (a) fat (b) bodiless (c) very thin (d) harmful
25. contumely   (a) contempt (b) charity (c) unhappiness (d) bliss
26. melancholy   (a) anger (b) fear (c) sadness (d) laughter
27. felicity   (a) love (b) happiness (c) clumsiness (d) fatigue
28. infallible   (a) incapable of error (b) clumsy (c) mistaken (d) lost
29. exhort   (a) leave (b) enter (c) scream (d) urge
30. dearth   (a) vegetation (b) strength (c) graveyard (d) scarcity

4. Julius Caesar

cogitation
indifferent
encompass
loath
surly
ghastly
portentous
augment
insurrection
affable
valiant
imminent
cognizance
emulate
redress

puissant
unassailable
vouchsafe
havoc
inter
covert
testy
covetous
cynic
apparition
exigency
presage
disconsolate
misconstrue
tarry

Learn these words from *Julius Caesar*. Set I

1. *cogitation* (koj ih TAY shun) n. serious and careful thought, consideration, meditation
Sherlock Holmes would cogitate (KOJ ih tayt) on puzzling crimes. My friend is a cogitator (KOJ ih tay tor) who ponders the questions where did we come from, where are we going, and for what purpose are we here. In the battle of brains versus brawn, the human species demonstrates the triumph of cogitative (KOJ ih tay tiv) faculties over brute strength. Serious thinking is hard work; some people would do almost anything to avoid cogitation.

2. *indifferent* (in DIF ur unt) adj. unconcerned; having no preference or impartial; not particularly good or bad, mediocre
I am indifferent about which film to see; you make the choice. An indifferent student passes courses but is not outstanding.

3. *encompass* (en KUM pus) v. contain, surround, encircle
A high fence encompasses the mansion and its lawn. Her encyclopedic mind encompassed such vast knowledge that she would be an ideal quiz show contestant.

4. *loath* (LOHTH—rhymes with "both") adj. reluctant, unwilling, averse
Although the job pays well, I am loath to accept it since I will have to spend much time away from my family. Do not confuse "loath" with "loathe" (rhymes with "clothe" as in "I will clothe you in a mink coat") which means "dislike intensely, hate, detest." Because I loathe my obnoxious, parasitic, slovenly brother-in-law, I am loath to comply with my wife's suggestion that we invite him to our home for the weekend.

5. *surly* (SUR lee) adj. bad-tempered, cross, rude, gruff, uncivil
The soldiers loathed their sergeant who had the surly disposition of a junkyard dog.

6. *ghastly* (GAST lee) adj. horrible or frightfully shocking; deathlike in appearance, especially pale as a ghost; extremely unpleasant
The severed head, disemboweled heart, and absent thumbs of the corpse signified this was another ghastly crime of the serial killer. When Shakespeare's tyrant Macbeth holds a feast after having his companion

Banquo murdered, a ghastly vision of Banquo appears at the feast to terrorize Macbeth.

7. *portentous* (por TEN tus) adj. foreshadowing, warning, foreboding, ominous
As the new king received his crown, a portentous flash of lightening in the courtyard split a majestic oak in half, foreshadowing the civil war that would destroy his kingdom. In other words, the lightning was a portent (POR tent) or omen. In the Bible, Joseph explains that the Pharaoh's dreams portend (por TEND) seven years of abundant harvests followed by seven years of famine.

8. *augment* (awg MENT) v. make or become greater; increase; enlarge
Fertilizer augments agricultural production. Lies cause the augmentation (awg men TAY shun) of Pinocchio's nose.

9. *insurrection* (in suh REK shun) n. uprising or outbreak against established authority; rebellion, revolution, insurgence
The dictator ruthlessly crushed the insurrection and executed all the captured insurrectionists.

10. *affable* (AF uh bul) adj. pleasant, friendly, sociable, amiable
We associate an affable personality more with a social director than a drill sergeant. The boss cared not about the foreman's affability but his productivity.

Working With Words

Complete the following sentences by using each of the following words only once: cogitation, indifferent, encompass, loath, surly, ghastly, portentous, augment, insurrection, affable.

1. We witnessed a _____ sight of wrecked cars and mangled bodies on the highway.

2. I am _____ to send my child to an overnight camp unless I am assured he is under proper supervision.

3. Her _____ nature makes it easy for her to make new friends.

4. Although she claimed she was _____ and could not care less, I knew that my wife disliked that my former girlfriend was now working in my office.

5. The outbreak of war caused the country to _____ its production of fighter planes, tanks, and battle ships.

6. Whereas one brother is kind and affable, the other brother is mean and _____.

7. Nat Turner led an _____ of slaves in 1831 in Virginia until he was caught and executed.

8. Geniuses like Isaac Newton and Albert Einstein awe us with their powers of _____.

9. We all felt comfort and security when our mother would _____ us in her arms.

10. In Shakespeare's time heavenly occurrences like shooting stars were regarded as _____ signs foretelling earthly events.

Match the word on the left with its definition.

____1. indifferent

____2. augment

____3. loath

____4. portentous

____5. affable

____6. insurrection

____7. encompass

____8. cogitation

____9. ghastly

____10. surly

a. deathlike in appearance

b. meditation

c. having no preference

d. reluctant

e. increase

f. warning, ominous

g. friendly

h. bad-tempered

i. rebellion

j. contain, surround, encircle

Words in context of *Julius Caesar*

Shakespeare's *Julius Caesar* takes place in Rome in 44 B.C. Julius Caesar has defeated the opposing forces of Pompey and rules the Roman Republic. However, some fear that he will abolish the republic by having himself crowned king. In order to prevent such an event, they conspire to assassinate Caesar. *Julius Caesar* portrays this overthrow and its effect on two of the chief conspirators, the honorable Brutus and the cunning Cassius.

As Caesar proceeds through Rome in a glorious procession, a soothsayer or predictor of the future tells him, "Beware the ides of March" [March 15]. Caesar unconcernedly shrugs off the remark. But as soon as Caesar leaves, two aristocrats—Brutus and Cassius—discuss matters that will precipitate events that will prove the truth of the soothsayer's prophecy.

Cassius asks Brutus why the latter has not been friendly to him recently. Brutus replies that his serious face stems from personal problems, not from any dissatisfaction with Cassius. Reassured, Cassius now reveals "thoughts of great value, worthy **cogitations**" that he has kept to himself. These **cogitations** or deep thoughts involve the growing popularity and power of Caesar. When Cassius asks if Brutus wants Caesar to be king, Brutus replies,

> I would not, Cassius; yet I love him well....
> What is it that you would impart to me?
> If it be aught toward the general good,
> Set honor in one eye and death i' the other,
> And I will look on both **indifferently**.

Brutus asks Cassius to impart his **cogitations**. If these thoughts concern the welfare of the country, then Brutus will look on them **indifferently** or impartially; Brutus says that he can be **indifferent** or unconcerned about death if it means acting for the public good because he loves honor more than he fears death.

Cassius then suggests something be done to stop Caesar:

> Men at some time are masters of their fates;
> The fault, dear Brutus, is not in our stars,
> But in ourselves, that we are underlings.

The astrological signs do not predestine our fates; we decide whether we allow ourselves to be servants. Cassius goes on to ask when could it be said of Rome "that her wide walks **encompassed** but one man." Never until now did one man grow so large that the wide walks or streets could **encompass** or contain no one else who could share the power to rule Rome. Brutus says that he sympathizes with these ideas, will reflect on them, and will meet Cassius again for further discussion.

At this point Caesar and his procession pass through. Noticing Cassius, Caesar remarks to his loyal and trusted friend Mark Antony,

> Yond Cassius has a lean and hungry look;
> He thinks too much; such men are dangerous.

Cassius' discussion with Brutus shows that Caesar judges accurately.

While Caesar moves on, Casca—another who conspires to overthrow Caesar—joins Brutus and Cassius. Casca tells them that three times today Mark Antony offered the crown of king to Caesar as the cheering crowd urged acceptance. Caesar refused to accept the crown, though as Casca says, "He was very **loath** to lay his fingers off it." Caesar was **loath** or very unwilling to decline the kingship, just as Casca is **loath** to see him become king. Before Brutus and Casca depart, they arrange to see Cassius the next day. Alone, Cassius muses that Brutus is honorable and loved by Caesar and confesses if he were Brutus there would be no way anyone could persuade him to assassinate Caesar. Cassius then says that he will write several letters in different handwritings all speaking of Rome's great esteem for Brutus and urging him to save the republic. He will throw these letters through Brutus's window.

Afterwards in the midst of a raging storm, Casca remarks to a senator that he met a slave whose arm blazed with fire but was not scorched, a **surly** or bad-tempered lion who merely glared at him and passed by, and

> ...a hundred **ghastly** women,
> Transformed with their fear, who swore they saw
> Men all in fire walk up and down the streets.

Casca interprets the dreadful storm and the strange events of the burning hand, **surly** lion, and **ghastly** or deathly pale women as "**portentous** things," signs of warning. Significantly, Caesar will come to the capitol the next day.

At his home, Brutus meditates on his talk with Cassius. Brutus admits that Caesar's reason has always so far controlled his passions. However, Brutus speculates that Caesar

> **...augmented**
> Would run to these and these extremities;
> And therefore think him as a serpent's egg
> Which, hatched, would, as his kind, grow mischievous,
> And kill him in his shell.

In other words, an **augmented** or even greater Caesar might abuse his power by committing tyrannical extremes. Better, therefore, to kill him now—as one would an evil serpent still in its eggshell—before he does these horrible wrongs.

These thoughts are interrupted as a servant delivers a letter. Brutus reads the contents:

> Brutus, thou sleepest; awake, and see thyself!
> ...Speak, strike, redress!

This letter urging him to remedy Rome's situation further intensifies Brutus's thinking. He has not slept since his talk with Cassius. Brutus states that between the inception of a dreadful scheme and the acting out of it is a hideous period during which he feels that his mental and emotional condition "suffers ... the nature of an **insurrection**" or uprising. His spirit is in turmoil.

A servant then announces that Cassius and some men whose faces are hid by their hats and cloaks are at the door. Brutus knows that these are the conspirators who plan to assassinate Caesar. He says that if they hide their faces at night, they will not be able to find a dark enough place to conceal their features during the day. Better they should hide the conspiracy "in smiles and **affability**" or friendliness to camouflage their purpose.

Learn these words from *Julius Caesar*: Set II

1. *valiant* (VAL yunt) adj. brave, courageous, heroic
We made a valiant effort to contain the forest fire. "Valor" (VAL ur) means "courage, bravery, heroism" as when soldiers receive the Distinguished Service Cross for valor in combat.

2. *imminent* (IM uh nunt) adj. likely to happen soon, impending
We evacuated the building immediately because of the threat of an imminent explosion. The approaching summer signaled the imminence of vacationers on the beaches.

3. *cognizance* (KOG nih zuns) n. conscious knowledge, awareness, notice
The passengers embarking on the *Titanic* (thought to be the safest ship of its time) in 1912 had no cognizance that it would tragically collide with an iceberg. The art professor asked me if I was cognizant that the painting adorning my living room was an original by the seventeenth-century Dutch artist Rembrandt and worth millions. In *Julius Caesar* "cognizance" means "emblem or badge of service" that makes one knowledgeable or aware of the status of its bearer.

4. *emulate* (EM yuh layt) v. imitate in an effort to equal or surpass
Emulation is the sincerest form of flattery. Youths emulate their sports heroes. "Emulate" stems from the Latin word for "rival"; therefore, we work to rival or surpass those we emulate. In *Julius Caesar* Shakespeare uses "emulation" to mean " jealous rivalry."

5. *redress* (rih DRES) v. set right, repair, or make up for; correct, remedy, compensate
The company sought to redress the employees who had inhaled toxic fumes during work by sincere apologies and huge bonuses. "Redress" is also a noun meaning "correction, remedy, compensation." When my neighbor's son failed to redress the damage to my fence that his car backed into, I sought redress from his parents. Because her employer failed to live up to the terms of their contract, the worker sought redress in the courts.

6. *puissant* (PWIS unt) adj. powerful, strong, mighty, potent
"Puissant" is now a mainly literary or poetic word. The English poet John Milton (1608-1674), best known for his epic poem *Paradise Lost* about Adam and Eve's fall from grace, used "puissant" in his classic essay *Areopagitica* which defended freedom of the press against censorship. In this essay, Milton states, "Methinks I see in my mind a noble and puissant nation rousing herself like a strong man after sleep." In *King Lear*, Shakespeare's play about an old man (King Lear) whose cruel daughters cause his death, a friend of Lear describes the old king's wretched condition,

> His grief grew puissant, and the strings of life
> Began to crack [i.e., his heart strings or heart began to fail].

Legends and myths describe the puissance of ancient heroes.

7. *unassailable* (un uh SAY luh bul) adj. undeniable, indisputable, incapable of proving wrong; not susceptible or vulnerable to attack, impregnable
Her argument was so logical and well-supported by relevant facts that it was unassailable. Shakespeare's villain Macbeth thinks his fortress unassailable but finds it overcome by enemy forces. His enemies who assailed or attacked the fortress unassailably proved that it was assailable or vulnerable to attack.

8. *vouchsafe* (vowch SAYF—first syllable rhymes with "ouch") v. grant or give, especially as doing a favor
The king vouchsafed an interview to the humble peasant.

9. *havoc* (HAV uk) n. great destruction or confusion
Natural forces such as tornadoes, hurricanes, and earthquakes cause havoc; human creations like oil spills, air pollution, and war also wreak havoc.

10. *inter* (in TUR—rhymes with "fur") v. place in a grave or tomb; bury
The Pharaohs were interred in pyramids.

Working With Words

Complete the following sentences by using each of the following words only once: valiant, imminent, cognizance, emulate, redress, puissant, unassailable, vouchsafe, havoc, inter.

1. For over a thousand years, people regarded the statements about the physical world by the ancient Greek philosopher Aristotle as _____ or indisputable truths; Shakespeare's contemporary the philosopher and statesman Francis Bacon advocated that observation and the scientific method—not ancient authority—should be the means to acquire knowledge of our material universe.

2. As the soldier pressed the point of his gun to my temple, I faced _____ death.

3. Everyone feared the _____ sorcerer whose spells could annihilate the entire town.

4. The French government decided to _____ the remains of Napoleon in a magnificent tomb.

5. The famous violinist decided to _____ free music lessons to the poor but gifted student.

6. Young writers often _____ the style of their favorite authors.

7. Robin Hood would _____ poor victims by giving them the money he stole from their rich persecutors.

8. The old boxer made a _____ attempt to remain on his feet as his younger, swifter, more powerful foe battered him relentlessly.

9. The chief executive explained that she had no _____ of any wrong doing in her corporation or she would have redressed it immediately.

10. The wild party created such _____ that neighbors called the police.

Match the word on the left with its definition.

___1. havoc	a. bury
___2. puissant	b. grant or give
___3. imminent	c. indisputable
___4. inter	d. powerful
___5. valiant	e. correct
___6. emulate	f. courageous
___7. redress	g. destruction
___8. vouchsafe	h. likcly to happen soon
___9. cognizance	i. imitate
___10. unassailable	j. awareness

Words in context of *Julius Caesar*

Cassius tells Brutus and the other conspirators that Mark Antony should be killed as well as Caesar. Brutus, however, says that Mark Antony can do no harm once Caesar is dead. Reluctantly, Cassius acquiesces.

The morning of March 15, the ides of March, Caesar's wife reports ominous signs that Caesar should not go to the capitol that day. Caesar dismisses the warning,

> Cowards die many times before their deaths;
> The **valiant** never taste of death but once.

Cowards fearfully anticipate their death many times, but the **valiant** or brave do not let such thoughts disturb them. However, when his wife continues her plea that he remain home, he decides not to go to the senate. A conspirator then enters ready to accompany Caesar to the capitol. Caesar says that his wife dreamed of his statue spouting blood in which many Romans came to bathe their hands and she interprets these dream events as omens of "evils **imminent**" or likely to happen soon. Therefore, he has agreed to her plea to stay at home. The conspirator says that the dream has been misinterpreted. The statue's spouting blood signifies Rome will be revived through Caesar's blood and the men bathing their hands means that great men will seek a **cognizance** or badge of distinction that they have served Caesar. Others will therefore be **cognizant** or aware of their contribution to Rome. The conspirator adds that it would be a joke if people knew that Caesar feared to go to the capital because of his wife's dreams. Caesar now decides to go to the senate.

A teacher of rhetoric waits near the capitol with a letter warning Caesar of the assassination plot. The teacher says,

> My heart laments that virtue cannot live
> Out of the teeth of **emulation**.

"**Emulation**" here has the old meaning of "jealous rivalry" rather than the modern one of "imitation." The teacher sadly comments that because of his virtues Caesar cannot escape the jealous threats of his rivals.

As Caesar approaches the capitol, the teacher attempts to give him the letter. Caesar, however, says he will not accept petitions in the street. He takes his seat in the senate and asks if there are any wrongs "that Caesar and his senate must **redress**?" A conspirator, Metellus Cimber, comes forward, kneels, and asks that his brother's condition be **redressed** or corrected. He addresses Caesar:

> Most high, most mighty, and most **puissant** Caesar,
> Metellus Cimber throws before thy seat
> A humble heart,—

but Caesar immediately cuts him off. Although indeed most **puissant** or powerful, Caesar tells Metellus that servile behavior will not be effective. Slavish humbleness will not make Caesar change his mind and allow Metellus's banished brother to return. Brutus and Cassius then support Metellus's request. However, Caesar remains firm in his decision. He explains that just as the North Star alone among stars remains unmoved, so he unique among men cannot be moved from his position:

> Yet in the number [of men] I do know but one
> That **unassailable** holds on his rank [maintains his position],
> Unshaked of motion; and that am I he.

Caesar no sooner says that his decision is **unassailable** or indisputable then the conspirators stab him, demonstrating that he is not **unassailable** or invulnerable to attack. He dies uttering '*Et tu, Brute* (Even you, Brutus)?"

Mark Antony's servant arrives and says,

> If Brutus will **vouchsafe** that Antony
> May safely come to him

and if Brutus will then explain why Caesar deserved death, then Antony will reconcile with Brutus. Brutus **vouchsafes** or grants Mark Antony safety and tells him that he will justify the assassination. Antony says he will be satisfied with a good explanation and asks that he be allowed to speak at Caesar's funeral. Cassius tells Brutus not to grant this request, but Brutus gives permission for Antony to speak after Brutus's funeral oration. When he is by himself, Antony vents his true feelings and says that bloody strife will be unleashed in Rome

> And Caesar's spirit, ranging for revenge...
> Shall in these confines [regions] with a monarch's voice

Cry "**Havoc**!" and let slip the dogs of war.

Antony prophesies the **havoc** or great destruction of civil war.
Brutus gives his speech, explains that Caesar was ambitious, and says,

> If [a friend of Caesar] demand why Brutus rose aginst Caesar,
> this is my answer: not that I loved Caesar less, but that I loved
> Rome more.

The crowd cheers his speech. As Brutus leaves, he asks the people to stay and hear Mark Antony. Antony begins,

> Friends, Romans, countrymen, lend me your ears;
> I come to bury Caesar, not to praise him.
> The evil that men do lives after them,
> The good is oft **interred** with their bones.

Antony makes sure that the good deeds of Caesar do not remain **interred** or buried with his corpse. He vividly describes Caesar's great love and service to Rome. In this magnificent speech, Antony turns the crowd against Brutus and the other conspirators. Brutus and Cassius flee Rome to escape the raging mob.

Learn these words from *Julius Caesar.* Set III

1. *covert* (KOH vurt) adj. secret, hidden, concealed, disguised
Spies engage in covert activities. The opposite of "covert" is "overt" (OH vurt), meaning "open, unconcealed." Whereas some fraternities have covert or secret practices for the initiated, our group is completely overt and hides nothing from the public.

2. *testy* (TES tee) adj. easily annoyed, irritable, short-tempered, irascible
Waiting in long lines and being put on hold on the telephone make me testy.

3. *covetous* (KUV it us) adj. enviously and greedily desiring what is another's; greedy, avaricious
Covetous people never have enough. The Ten Commandments forbid covetousness: "You shall not covet your neighbor's house; you shall not covet your neighbor's wife, or his manservant or his maidservant, or his ox, or his ass, or anything that is your neighbor's." Although "covet," "covetous," and "covetousness" all have to do with wrongful greed, the adjective "coveted" often does not imply anything wrong but merely means "highly desirable or sought after" as when one refers to the coveted Nobel Prize.

4. *cynic* (SIN ik) n. one who doubts the goodness and sincerity of human motives
Cynics doubt that we ever help people without expecting something in return. Cynical remarks are skeptical, distrustful, or ironic. The Victorian playwright Oscar Wilde described a cynic as a "man who knows the price of everything, and the value of nothing"; perhaps the playwright was being cynical about cynicism.

5. *apparition* (ap uh RISH un) n. sudden or unusual appearance; ghost, phantom, specter
When Hamlet sees his father's ghost, the apparition says that he was murdered by Hamlet's uncle.

6. *exigency* (EK suh jun see) n. situation demanding immediate attention or action; urgency, emergency
In the emergency room of a hospital, physicians deal constantly with exigencies. When our water pipes burst, we called a plumber to handle the

exigency. The adjective form is "exigent"; exigent situations demand immediate attention. In *Julius Caesar*, however, Shakespeare uses "exigent" as a noun meaning "emergency."

7. *presage* (PRES ij) n. sign, warning, omen, presentiment; v. foretell, warn, predict, foreshadow
April showers presage May flowers. My empty stomach is a presage that it's dinner time. Declining sales are a presage that workers will be discharged.

8. *disconsolate* (dis KON suh lit) adj. hopelessly sad, downcast, inconsolable, forlorn
After his wife died, our neighbor was disconsolate.

9. *misconstrue* (mis kun STROO) v. misinterpret
I misconstrued his smile as approval and sympathy when really he was laughing at me. I correctly construed or interpreted the rattlesnake's warning; if I had misconstrued the warning, the misconstruction could have cost me my life. In *Julius Caesar*, the senator Cicero says that "men may construe things after their fashion [i.e., in their own way]" that totally misconstrues what the things really mean.

10. *tarry* (TAR ee) v. delay, linger, wait; stay in a place temporarily, sojourn
Hurry Harry, don't tarry. We tarried some days in Paris before we continued our trip to Germany.

Working With Words

Complete the following sentences by using each of the following words only once: covert, testy, covetous, cynic, apparition, exigency, presage, disconsolate, misconstrue, tarry.

1. Hearing excuses why tenants cannot pay their rent makes the real estate manager irritable or _____ .

2. The _____ did not believe that anyone would help another without expecting something in return.

3. You look as _____ as if you had just lost your best friend.

4. I made myself perfectly clear so no one would _____ my meaning.

5. The public did not know of the _____ operation to build an atomic bomb during World War II.

6. We invited the weary travelers to _____ with us awhile before they resumed their long journey.

7. Do you believe that a crystal ball can _____ the future?

8. Many scholars think that Shakespeare himself played the _____ or ghost of Hamlet's father.

9. The _____ miser became testy whenever I mentioned someone richer than himself.

10. My intelligent, practical, decisive wife could cope with any _____ .

Match the word on the left with its definition.

____1. testy   a. sad
____2. tarry   b. ghost
____3. presage   c. doubter of human goodness
____4. exigency   d. linger
____5. covetous   e. irritable
____6. covert   f. secret
____7. cynic   g. misinterpret
____8. apparition   h. enviously greedy
____9. misconstrue   i. predict
____10. disconsolate   j. emergency

Words in context of *Julius Caesar*

Antony forms an alliance with Octavius and Lepidus against Brutus and Cassius. Antony tells Octavius,

> And let us presently go sit in council,
> How **covert** matter may be best disclosed,
> And open perils surest answered.

They will discuss how **covert** or hidden matters will be revealed and how obvious dangers will best be met.

Meanwhile, Brutus and Cassius argue about the affairs of their army. Brutus accuses Cassius of taking bribes. When Cassius responds with anger, Brutus says, "Must I stand and crouch under your **testy** humor?" Brutus asks if he must endure Cassius's irritable temper. He says that when he needed money to pay his soldiers and sent to Cassius for gold, Cassius denied him. Brutus then exclaims that if he ever "grows so **covetous**" or greedy as Cassius as to hoard money "from his friend," then "be ready, gods, with all your thunderbolts" to "dash [Brutus] to pieces." Cassius then says he loves Brutus who now hates him, bares his breast while giving his dagger to Brutus, and tells Brutus to plunge it into his naked breast. This dramatic gesture conciliates Brutus. At this point, a poet who has heard them arguing enters their tent in order to reconcile them:

> Love, and be friends, as two such men should be;
> For I have seen more years, I'm sure than ye.

Cassius laughs at the poet's lines and says, "How viley does this **cynic** rhyme!" In ancient times the **cynics** were philosophers; from them comes the word "**cynic**" with its modern meaning of "one who doubts the goodness and sincerity of human motives." However, Cassius uses the word merely to mean "philosopher" when he says that this **cynic** is an awful poet. Brutus and Cassius, already reconciled, drive him from the tent.

That night the ghost of Julius Caesar visits Brutus who exclaims,

> Who comes here?
> I think it is the weakness of mine eyes
> That shapes this monstrous **apparition**.

It comes upon me. Art thou any thing?
Art thou some god, some angel, or some devil,
That makest my blood cold and my hair to stare?

The **apparition** or ghost says that he will visit Brutus at the battle of Philippi and then vanishes.

At Philippi, Antony and Octavius prepare to meet the army of Brutus and Cassius. Antony directs Octavius to lead the battle on the left side of the field. Octavius refuses and says he will the lead forces on the right, Antony on the left. Antony then asks, "Why do you cross me in this **exigent**?" Octavius says he is not opposing Antony in this **exigency** or urgent situation; none the less, Octavius maintains that he will lead the forces on the right. Octavius, quite a bit younger than Antony, stubbornly asserts himself against the commands of his more experienced comrade.

As Cassius gets ready to lead his troops against them, he expresses his doubts about the imminent battle. Formerly, Cassius thought it mere superstition to trust in omens, but he says,

Now I change my mind,
And partly credit things that do **presage**.

Cassius feels that the departure of two eagles that had flown above his army as it advanced to Philippi with their recent replacement by ravens and crows **presages** or foretells disaster.

Antony's troops then surround Cassius's army. Cassius sends a messenger to find out whether soldiers in the distance are friend or foe. Cassius then asks his slave Pindarus to climb a hill and report on the progress of the messenger. Pindarus sees the messenger dismount in the midst of a group of roaring soldiers. The slave wrongly assumes that enemies have captured the messenger and reports this news to Cassius. Thinking that all is lost, Cassius, rather than become a prisoner, gives his sword to Pindarus and asks the slave to kill him.

The messenger returns to see Cassius—whom he left "all **disconsolate**" or hopelessly sad—dead. The messenger had actually met Brutus's soldiers after they had beaten Octavius's forces and had dismounted amidst their victorious cheers. Looking down on Cassius, the messenger realizes, "Alas, thou hast **misconstrued** everything." Cassius committed suicide because he **misconstrued** or misinterpreted victory as defeat.

The tide of war changes again and Antony defeats Brutus's forces. Like Cassius, Brutus also is unwilling to be taken prisoner. Brutus says,

> Our enemies have beat us to the pit.
> It is more worthy to leap in ourselves
> Than **tarry** till they push us.

Rather than **tarry** or wait to be captured, Brutus gives his sword to his servant, asks him to hold it steady, and then impales himself on it. The victorious Octavius and Antony arrive on the scene. Antony looks down on Brutus, and with forgiveness, respect, and admiration for his adversary, eulogizes,

> This was the noblest Roman of them all.

REVIEW EXERCISE
Select the definition closest in meaning.

1. indifferent   (a) unsure   (b) positive   (c) angry   (d) unconcerned
2. disconsolate   (a) sad   (b) peaceful   (c) aggressive   (d) indecisive
3. cynic   (a) loser   (b) winner   (c) doubter   (d) impostor
4. vouchsafe   (a) grant   (b) withhold   (c) hide   (d) discover
5. inter   (a) bury   (b) uphold   (c) alphabetize   (d) confuse
6. ghastly   (a) pleasant   (b) horrible   (c) false   (d) confusing
7. cogitation   (a) effort   (b) thought   (c) journey   (d) homecoming
8. augment   (a) hurt   (b) slander   (c) enlarge   (d) remove
9. presage   (a) foretell   (b) meditate   (c) heal   (d) bury
10. tarry   (a) hurry   (b) carry   (c) remove   (d) delay
11. loath   (a) unwilling   (b) living   (c) sleeping   (d) eager
12. valiant   (a) fearful   (b) skillful   (c) brave   (d) impartial
13. cognizance   (a) awareness   (b) hatred   (c) effort   (d) strength
14. redress   (a) repair   (b) ruin   (c) confuse   (d) steal
15. testy   (a) happy   (b) eager   (c) short-tempered   (d) dull
16. encompass   (a) sail   (b) guide   (c) hike   (d) surround
17. unassailable   (a) weak   (b) unable to be attacked   (c) unfit   (d) slow
18. covert   (a) concealed   (b) common   (c) open   (d) clever
19. portentous   (a) smooth   (b) ominous   (c) funny   (d) wasted
20. affable   (a) handsome   (b) ugly   (c) pleasant   (d) irritable
21. emulate   (a) recognize   (b) travel   (c) imitate   (d) despise
22. misconstrue   (a) misinterpret   (b) avoid   (c) lie   (d) meditate
23. surly   (a) happy   (b) bad-tempered   (c) friendly   (d) lively
24. insurrection   (a) rebellion   (b) burial   (c) damage   (d) agreement
25. apparition   (a) celebration   (b) graduation   (c) ghost   (d) hero
26. exigency   (a) royalty   (b) loss   (c) emergency   (d) departure
27. imminent   (a) impending   (b) prominent   (c) unknown   (d) fierce
28. puissant   (a) cowardly   (b) powerful   (c) weak   (d) consistent
29. havoc   (a) error   (b) agreement   (c) destruction   (d) luck
30. covetous   (a) generous   (b) sociable   (c) clever   (d) greedy

5. Othello

obsequious
lascivious
iniquity
mountebank
conjure
overt
alacrity
discern
descry
egregious
bestial
inordinate
dilatory
politic
ruminate

filch
surmise
inference
tranquil
castigate
venial
lethargy
construe
censure
peevish
restitution
pernicious
amorous
extenuate
malice

Learn these words from *Othello*: Set I

1. *obsequious* (ub SEE kwee us) adj. excessively attentive, flattering, or obedient in order to gain favor; servile, fawning
At his birthday party, the rich landowner found the insincere flattery and obsequious behavior of his relatives repulsive.

2. *lascivious* (luh SIV ee us) adj. lustful, lewd
Lascivious illustrations accompanied the pornographic text. Are you familiar with the lascivious Wife of Bath in Chaucer's *The Canterbury Tales*?

3. *iniquity* (in IK wuh tee) n. great wickedness or injustice
When President Franklin Delano Roosevelt said, "This is a day that will live in infamy," he was referring to the iniquitous Japanese bombing of Pearl Harbor on December 7, 1941. The destruction of New York City's Twin Towers in the World Trade Center on September 11, 2001, was another act of iniquity.

4. *mountebank* (MOUNT uh bank) n. deceiver who falsely claims to have knowledge or skill; impostor, swindler, fraud, charlatan
"Mountebank" stems from Italian origin when frauds and swindlers in medieval Italy would mount (*monta*) a bench (*banco*) in the public square, provide entertainment to attract a crowd, and proceed to sell the spectators worthless goods. Promoters of fad diets and gadgets which claim to condition and transform the body effortlessly are mountebanks.

5. *conjure* (KON jur) v. summon by a spell or magic; practice magic; imagine, invent
The great American magician Harry Houdini (1874-1926) exposed mountebanks who claimed the power to conjure departed souls. "Conjure up" means to "make appear as if by magic, imagine, invent." We all know someone who continually conjures up schemes to get rich quickly. A conjurer can be either a magician or a sorcerer.

6. *overt* (oh VURT) adj. openly done, unconcealed, not secret
When his overseer tried to grab the slave Frederick Douglass (1817-1895) for a whipping, Douglass—later to become the most prominent African American leader of his time—overtly defied the overseer by seizing his throat and beating him up. "Covert," an antonym for "overt,"

means "not openly done, concealed, secret." Declaration of war is an overt action; spy activities are covert.

7. *alacrity* (uh LAK rih tee) n. cheerful, quick, or eager readiness and liveliness; briskness, sprightliness
Whenever I open a can of cat food, my cat runs to me with alacrity.

8. *discern* (dih SURN) v. perceive, distinguish
Eagles can discern distant objects better than humans; hence the term "eagle eye" for keen eyesight. The telescope made the craters of the moon easily discernible. Shakespeare was a discerning or insightful observer of human nature.

9. *descry* (dih SCRY) v. catch sight of, discover, detect
Whereas "discern" can be used in a mental or physical sense, "descry" is limited to the physical. A careful reader of Shakespeare can discern—not descry—his play on words and his subtle and complex description of character. Hamlet descries or discerns the Ghost at the beginning of the play but cannot at this time discern with certainty whether it is a benevolent or evil spirit. A sailor would climb to the crow's nest near the top of the ship's mast to descry land or other vessels.

10. *egregious* (ih GREE jus) adj. outstandingly bad
An egregious engineering miscalculation caused the newly constructed skyscraper to topple during the season's first hurricane. The principal fired the teacher for egregiously missing many classes, showing up drunk for others, and accepting payment for grades.

Working With Words

Complete the following sentences by using each of the following words only once: obsequious, lascivious, iniquity, mountebank, conjure, overt, alacrity, discern, descry, egregious.

1. Three witches _____ up a vision that appalls Macbeth.

2. We crave genuine appreciation but dislike _____ flattery.

3. The boos and hisses of the audience displayed its _____ dislike of the play.

4. The egregiously incompetent theater critic could not _____ a poor play from a masterpiece.

5. My teacher told me that I am such an _____ speller that she is surprised when I correctly write my name.

6. With the aid of a telescope in 1610, the Italian astronomer and physicist Galileo was the first to _____ the four largest moons of Jupiter.

7. Our best physics major shockingly revealed that she earned her college tuition by posing for _____ photographs.

8. I had been fooled so many times by false advertising that I thought every salesperson a _____.

9. In *Hamlet*, Claudius's murder of his own brother is an act of _____.

10. When my mother announced that the Christmas feast was ready, we ran to the table with _____.

Match the word on the left with its definition.

___1. mountebank   a. lustful, lewd
___2. alacrity   b. openly done
___3. discerning   c. outstandingly bad
___4. obsequious   d. swindler, charlatan
___5. egregious   e. perceptive
___6. conjure   f. catch sight of
___7. descry   g. wickedness
___8. overt   h. servile, fawning
___9. lascivious   i. summon by magic or a spell
___10. iniquity   j. cheerful eagerness, quickness

Words in context of *Othello*

Race, jealousy, and villainy pervade the intense tragedy *Othello* that culminates in the hero's killing the woman whom he loves more than life itself. Othello, a black man who serves as general of the army that defends the city of Venice, Italy, marries a young, beautiful white woman of high social position named Desdemona. His satanic officer Iago plants the seeds of doubt in Othello's mind regarding the fidelity of Desdemona. This craftiest and most subtle of Shakespeare's villains cultivates these seeds until they flower into insane jealousy.

As the play opens, Iago—the ensign or soldier who carries the army's banner into battle—talks with Roderigo, a Venetian gentleman who loves Desdemona. The ensign seethes that he, a seasoned soldier who has many times showed his valor in Othello's wars, has been bypassed by Othello who has selected Cassio to be his lieutenant or second-in-command. Iago has no respect for dutiful servants who enjoy their "**obsequious** bondage" and when they are old are dismissed with nothing. Rather, he respects servants who, though seemingly **obsequious** or excessively attentive and obedient, in actuality cheat their masters. The ensign declares himself such a schemer in regard to Othello. Iago and Roderigo then come to the house of Brabantio, a Venetian senator, and tell him that Othello has eloped with his daughter Desdemona. In the process, they cast racial slurs on Othello, referring to him as "thick-lips," "an old black ram," "a **lascivious** Moor"—a lustful Moor or African (technically Moors were from north Africa but Shakespeare's European contemporaries often thought of Moors as Africans in general).

Iago then meets with Othello and says that he was about to kill someone for slandering the general. Iago says that if not for his lacking the **iniquity** or wickedness to kill anyone other than in war, he would have stabbed the slanderer. Cassio arrives and announces that the Duke has summoned Othello to an emergency meeting concerning a Turkish invasion of Cyprus, an island in the Mediterranean controlled by Venice. At this point Brabantio comes upon them and accuses Othello of using magic to enchant his daughter. However, when the senator learns where Othello must go, he accompanies the general to the Duke's council.

There Brabantio accuses Othello of using "spells and medicines bought of **mountebanks**" or frauds and having **conjured** or cast a magic spell on Desdemona. Surely, in this white society of Venice, his much sought after daughter would not be attracted to this hideous black man. The Duke says that accusation is no proof and that a "more **overt** test" or obvious evidence is needed. Othello explains that Brabantio often invited him to his house. In those more amiable times the senator questioned him about his life's story. Othello told of such marvelous adventures that Desdemona said that these stories would woo a woman. Taking his cue, Othello professed his love and Desdemona reciprocated. While Desdemona is sent for to settle the dispute between the senator and the general, Othello proclaims his "natural and prompt **alacrity**" or eager readiness to endure the necessary hardships for the coming war against the Turks. Desdemona then arrives and confirms her husband Othello's account of their courtship. Embittered, Brabantio leaves with these words,

> Look to her, Moor, if thou has eyes to see.
> She has deceived her father, and may thee.

After everyone else leaves, Iago tells Roderigo that he will still help him to get Desdemona. When Roderigo also departs leaving only Iago on stage, Iago lets the audience know that he thinks Roderigo a fool. Iago will use him for his own revenge on Othello. Not only does the soldier hate Othello for favoring Cassio, but Iago's warped mind also wrongly suspects that his wife Emilia—Desdemona's attendant and friend—has slept with Othello. Iago contemplates how he will make Othello believe that Cassio and Desdemona are lovers.

The scene moves to Cyprus during a raging storm as Montano, who is the governor of the island, and his men await Othello's fleet. Montano asks what anyone can "**discern** at sea." One of his men answers that he can **discern** or perceive nothing; so uproarious are the seas in this dreadful storm that he can nowhere between heaven and earth "**descry** a sail" or catch sight of any of Othello's ships. Cassio's ship then arrives with the comforting news that the tempest has destroyed most of the Turkish fleet, thus reducing the threat of invasion. Soon after, Iago, Desdemona, Emilia, and Roderigo sail into port. Finally, to the great relief of those on the island, Othello arrives.

Once they are alone, Iago tells Roderigo that Desdemona secretly loves Cassio. Therefore, Roderigo should find a way to provoke a fight with Cassio who will stand watch this night. The brawl will cause Cassio to be dismissed by Othello for breach of discipline. With Cassio out of the way, Roderigo will then succeed with Desdemona. The gullible Roderigo agrees to the plan.

No sooner does Roderigo leave, then Iago muses on his revenge. He concedes,

> The Moor—howbeit [although] that I endure him not—
> Is of a constant, loving, noble nature,
> And, I dare think, he'll prove to Desdemona
> A most dear husband.

These lines assure us that Othello is indeed a noble, loyal, and loving soul since his qualities are acknowledged by his worst enemy. Nonetheless, Iago confesses once again that he fears Othello has slept with Emilia and now also reveals that he suspects that Emilia has deceived him with Cassio as well. If Iago's plan succeeds, he will

> Make the Moor thank me, love, and reward me
> For making him **egregiously** an ass,
> And practicing upon his peace and quiet,
> Even to madness.

Othello will thank Iago as the general becomes an **egregious** or outstandingly bad fool through insane jealousy.

Learn these words from *Othello*: Set II

1. *bestial* (BES chul) adj. like a beast; brutish, inhuman, savage, brutal
Raised by apes in Africa, Tarzan appeared bestial to Western explorers in Africa. However, when Tarzan first witnessed the cruelty of mutinous sailors, he judged them as far more bestial, brutal, and cruel than the animals of the jungle.

2. *inordinate* (in OR din it) adj. exceeding proper limits; excessive, immoderate; not regulated or irregular
Aunt Sarah satisfied her inordinate desire for sweets by gorging on boxes of chocolate. Iago causes Othello to become inordinately jealous of Desdemona.

3. *dilatory* (DIL uh tor ee) adj. delaying, slow, tardy, procrastinating
Joan jumps to every task with energy and alacrity; her dilatory sister will never do today what she can put off till tomorrow.

4. *politic* (POL ih tik) adj. shrewdly tactful, prudent, expedient
When my teacher inquired why I was giving him a long explanation when asking for an extension on my late paper, I replied that I was being polite; he said I was not being polite but politic.

5. *ruminate* (ROO muh nayt) v. chew the cud; meditate, ponder, muse
A ruminant is an animal such as cow or deer that chews its cud (i.e., brings up food from its stomach to chew again slowly). Hence, when we ruminate we ponder or chew on our thoughts. Sometimes we replay a scene in our minds and ruminate on it to such an extent that it becomes difficult to free ourselves from obsessive thoughts.

6. *filch* (FILCH) v. steal, especially something of small value; pilfer
Many employees do not consider it stealing when they filch small items like pens, pencils, paper clips, and envelopes.

7. *surmise* (sur MYZ) n. & v. guess, conjecture
From the smile on your face, I surmise you passed your driving test. Her surmises about the future proved so accurate that we believe she has supernatural abilities.

8. *inference* (IN fur uns) n. conclusion by reasoning from facts, evidence, premises; implication, guess, surmise
The detective said that there were too few clues to make any meaningful inferences about the identity of the murderer. From the grimace on my son's face as he swallows the medicine, I infer that he hates its taste.

9. *tranquil* (TRANG kwil) adj. peaceful, calm, quiet, undisturbed, serene
While all around her were agitated and excited, my mother alone maintained a tranquil mind. One of the aims of our Constitution is to "insure domestic tranquillity."

10. *castigate* (KAS tih gayt) v. severely punish, criticize, chastise, reprove
To castigate is to punish either physically or verbally in order to correct or improve. Before my father would castigate us, he would solemnly state, "Spare the rod and spoil the child." As you might surmise, what followed was physical or corporal castigation.

Working With Words

Complete the following sentences by using each of the following words only once: bestial, inordinate, dilatory, politic, ruminate, filch, surmise, inference, tranquil, castigate.

1. My sisters and I would _____ cookies from the cookie jar.

2. When Martin Luther King, Jr. spoke about the "paralysis of analysis," he meant we must no longer _____ about problems but act to solve them.

3. Exercise, sufficient sleep, and a clear conscience contribute to a _____ mind.

4. The honest doctor said that he could not forecast with precise accuracy how long a terminal patient would live; he could only _____.

5. Explorers often described strange people as _____ and brutish; of course, these people probably also regarded the explorers as not fully human.

6. The time for _____ tactics ended; we had to act decisively and immediately.

7. Every word and gesture of the shrewd diplomat was _____, designed to achieve his goals.

8. Iago's _____ desire for revenge results in his devilishly cruel torture of Othello.

9. When Othello sees his wife's handkerchief in his officer's hand, he makes the false _____ that his wife and the officer are lovers.

10. The kindly coach would _____ us in private, thus sparing us public humiliation.

Match the word on the left with its definition.

___1. ruminate
___2. infer
___3. inordinate
___4. filch
___5. bestial
___6. tranquil
___7. dilatory
___8. surmising
___9. politic
___10. castigate

a. pilfer, steal
b. serene, peaceful
c. like a beast; brutal, savage
d. conjecturing, guessing
e. chastise, reprove, punish
f. procrastinating, tardy, delaying
g. conclude by reasoning from facts
h. muse, ponder, meditate
i. excessive, immoderate
j. expedient, prudent, tactful

Words in context of *Othello*

While Othello and Desdemona enjoy their wedding night and the island community celebrates their nuptials, Iago coaxes a reluctant Cassio—who guards these festivities and knows his low tolerance for alcohol—to drink. As planned, Cassio gets drunk and Roderigo provokes him into a fight. When governor Montano tries to restrain Cassio, Cassio wounds him as well. The tumult arouses Othello who demands to know what happened. With feigned hesitancy for fear of injuring a friend's honor, the consummate villain Iago describes Cassio's misbehavior. To enforce order on the island, Othello makes an example of Cassio by stripping him of his lieutenancy.

Left with Iago, Cassio mourns that he has lost his reputation, "the immortal part of myself, and what remains is **bestial**" or brutish. He berates himself for getting drunk, declaring that "every **inordinate** cup is unblessed and the ingredience [ingredients] is a devil." He blames **inordinate** or excessive drink for his troubles, but the real devil is Iago. Iago tells him that reputation is a meaningless illusion, often "got without merit and lost without deserving." This superb villain then consoles Cassio by telling him to ask Desdemona to help him get back in Othello's good graces. When Cassio leaves, Iago plans to persuade Othello that Desdemona pleads for Cassio because she lusts for the former lieutenant.

Roderigo meets Iago and complains of suffering a beating from Cassio and having spent almost all his money. He will return to Venice. Iago soothes him and urges him to be patient because they are not working by witchcraft but by intelligence which "depends on **dilatory** time," on the slow passing of time for their plan to unfold successfully. Iago further explains that the small hurt received by Roderigo resulted in Cassio's dismissal. He sends the reassured Roderigo away and schemes how he will bring Othello at exactly the right moment to find Cassio asking Desdemona for a favor.

Cassio comes to Dedemona to ask her help in getting back his position. Desdemona explains that Othello will maintain "a **politic**" distance, that is a politically necessary or expedient unfriendliness toward Cassio for only as long as necessary. In the meantime, Desdemona will continuously advocate Cassio's reinstatement. She reassures Cassio that he will soon be restored to friendship with Othello.

Cassio departs from Desdemona just as Othello and Iago enter. Othello catches sight of Cassio and Iago mutters, "I like not that," noting that it is strange for Cassio to sneak away so guiltily as Othello approaches. He has planted his seed of doubt regarding Desdemona's fidelity in Othello's mind. No sooner does Desdemona greet Othello, then she begins pleading Cassio's case until good-naturedly Othello promises her he will do as she wishes. As Desdemona exits, Iago implies but never directly states that something is going on between Cassio and Desdemona. His implications are bait that hook Othello because the general then tells his ensign to speak

> As thou dost **ruminate**, and give thy worst of thoughts
> The worst of words.

Othello asks Iago to disclose his **ruminations** or meditations and not hold back on his worst suspicions. Of course, Iago plays his game superbly and begs that he not share what are probably fabrications from an overly distrustful mind. Without strong evidence, he will certainly not injure anyone's reputation.

> Good name in man and woman, dear my lord,
> Is the immediate jewel of their souls.
> Who steals my purse, steals trash; 'tis something, nothing;
> 'Twas mine, 'tis his, and has been slave to thousands:
> But he that **filches** from me my good name
> Robs me of that which not enriches him
> And makes me poor indeed.

Whereas earlier Iago told Cassio that reputation was a false, trivial, and meaningless illusion, he now tells Othello that he will not **filch** or steal someone's good name for reputation is the most precious jewel we possess. Othello responds as Iago hopes and demands to know his ensign's ruminations. Iago tells him, "O beware, my lord, of jealousy." Othello asserts that he is devoid of jealousy and will not make inflated **surmises** or unfounded, exaggerated guesses corresponding to Iago's **inferences** or deductions. Iago says that he is glad that Othello does not have a jealous nature, and with almost the same breath adds that Desdemona "did deceive her father, marrying you," echoing Brabantio's farewell warning to the general. The hook of jealousy has fastened on Othello's heart.

As Iago leaves, Desdemona enters. Othello complains of a headache and Desdemona tries to put her handkerchief around his forehead to ease his pain. Othello pushes the handkerchief away and Desdemona drops it. When Othello and Desdemona exit, Emilia enters, picks up the handkerchief, and brings it to her husband, who had often asked her to filch it for him. Iago then plants the handkerchief in Cassio's living quarters.

Othello later appears with Iago and wails, "Farewell the **tranquil** mind." Never again will Othello know **tranquillity** or peace of mind. He threatens Iago unless the ensign gives him visual proof of Desdemona's infidelity. Iago says that it would be impossible to witness them in the act of love. He then fabricates how in the barracks when he was lying awake next to the sleeping Cassio, Cassio while dreaming out loud embraced Iago—thinking him Desdemona—and spoke of how Othello must never know of their adulterous affair. Iago tells Othello that he has seen Cassio with Desdemona's handkerchief. Now convinced that Desdemona is unfaithful, Othello commands Iago to kill Cassio within three days.

When Othello next meets Desdemona, he takes her palm and says that it signifies a need for fasting, prayer, and "**castigation**" (here meaning "discipline" rather than its modern meaning of "punishment"). He then asks for his handkerchief. Desdemona says she does not have it now but will get it later. Othello explains that the handkerchief was woven by an Egyptian sorceress who told Othello's mother that as long as his mother kept this handkerchief she would always have the love of Othello's father. But if she lost it or gave it away, her husband would loathe her. The more Othello asks for the handkerchief, the more Desdemona puts off his request and counters with her request for Cassio's restoration to Othello's good graces. Furious, Othello storms out in a jealous rage. Shortly thereafter Cassio gives this handkerchief to a prostitute named Bianca.

Learn these words from *Othello*: Set III

1. *venial* (VEE nee ul, VEEN yul) adj. pardonable, forgivable, excusable; not serious, minor, trivial
In the Roman Catholic Church, a "venial sin" is minor and does not remove the soul from God's grace, whereas a "mortal sin" deprives the soul of God's grace and causes damnation. In a general sense, "venial" refers to a minor offense. Coming back to your car a few minutes after the parking meter has expired is a venial traffic violation. Accidentally spilling water on someone at lunch is a venial offense. Do not confuse "venial" (which comes from the Latin word for "forgivable") with "venal" (VEE nul, from the Latin word "for sale") which means "corruptible, open to bribery." A venal public health official who endangers the community by accepting money to ignore health regulations commits a major—not a venial—crime.

2. *lethargy* (LETH ur jee) n. laziness, sluggishness, drowsiness, lack of energy
"Lethargy" comes from the Greek mythological river Lethe that would wipe out the memories of departed souls before they entered Hades, the region of the dead. Lazy, sluggish individuals displaying lethargy seem without memory of any motivating purpose. During the hot, hazy days of summer vacation I become lethargic.

3. *construe* (kun STROO) v. explain, interpret
I construed from the deep growl and baring of its fangs that the dog did not like me. I construe that my boss's smile means I will get my promotion. "Misconstrue" means "misunderstand, misjudge, misinterpret." Actually, when my boss fired me, I realized that I had misconstrued his smile.

4. *censure* (SEN shur) n. strong disapproval, harsh criticism, blame; v. disapprove, criticize, blame
The biblical lines "Why do you see the speck that is in your brother's eye, but not notice the log that is in your own?" and "Let him that is without sin among you be the first to throw a stone" warn us about censuring others if we do not censure ourselves for the same offenses. Even though the accused man was found not guilty in court, he could not escape public censure because most people still felt that he had committed the crime.

5. *peevish* (PEE vish) adj. irritable, fretful, cross, ill-tempered, querulous
Lack of a good night's sleep, stepping on a thumbtack while getting out of bed, and missing breakfast as she rushed off to the office accounted for her peevishness toward fellow workers. It peeves me when my children leave their dirty dishes scattered around the house for me to collect and wash. I never ask my father for the keys to his car when he is peevish.

6. *restitution* (res tih TOO shun) n. compensation for loss, damage, or injury; restoration of something to the rightful owner
I offered to make restitution for knocking over my neighbor's mailbox as I left his driveway. My kindly neighbor was satisfied with my sincere apology and wanted no further restitution. Can any restitution compensate for the loss of a loved one?

7. *pernicious* (pur NISH us) adj. very harmful, injurious, damaging, destructive, deadly
He committed suicide by sealing his garage, turning on the car engine, and inhaling the pernicious carbon monoxide fumes. We suffer from pernicious acts of religious intolerance and racial bigotry.

8. *amorous* (AM ur us) adj. pertaining to love, especially sexual love; loving
The amorous embraces of Romeo and Juliet contrast with the pernicious behavior of their feuding families. We exchange amorous greeting cards on Valentine's Day. The English poet Geoffrey Chaucer (1340-1400) first described the amorous custom of choosing sweethearts on Saint Valentine's Day.

9. *extenuate* (ik STEN yoo ayt) v. lessen the seriousness of
When learning of the extenuating circumstances of the student having to attend to his hospitalized mother, the teacher excused the student's absences. The lawyer attempted to extenuate her client's guilt by citing his youth, poverty, and dysfunctional upbringing.

10. *malice* (MAL iss) n. ill will, desire to harm others, spite
What is the motive of Iago's malicious behavior toward Othello? In theory, an impartial judge rather than the victim determines punishment for the offender because the former acts out of a sense of justice whereas the latter would be motivated by malice or revenge.

Working With Words

Complete the following sentences by using each of the following words only once: venial, lethargy, construe, censure, peevish, restitution, pernicious, amorous, extenuate, malice.

1. When normally enthusiastic and energetic Bob lost his job, his vitality faded into _____.

2. "Sticks and stones may break my bones, but names will never harm me" is not always true because degrading words can have a _____ or harmful effect on one's personality.

3. Do not _____ the manager's soft-spoken, kindly manner as weakness; he acts decisively to rid the company of incompetent employees.

4. Willing to accept full responsibility and punishment for his crime, the defendant said nothing to _____ his offense.

5. When my mother found out that I had lied by denying that I ate some cookies she prepared for a neighbor's party, she censured me by saying that filching some cookies is _____ or trivial but lying about it is not.

6. Although usually calm and serene, my father always became _____ when anyone suggested he quit the work he enjoyed to find a job that paid more.

7. The bonobo or pygmy chimpanzee is known as the _____ ape since it often reconciles disputes with mutually agreeable sexual behavior.

8. No amount of _____ can compensate me for the loss of my good name.

9. The saintly reformer felt no _____ toward his enemies, only a profound pity and compassion for them.

10. The librarian said that she may personally _____ or severely disapprove of certain books but she did not believe that anyone should censor or delete passages from them.

Match the word on the left with its definition.

___1. peevish   a. loving
___2. lethargy   b. harsh criticism
___3. venial   c. ill will
___4. restitution   d. lessen the seriousness of
___5. construe   e. trivial, forgivable
___6. censure   f. compensation, restoration
___7. extenuate   g. harmful, destructive, deadly
___8. amorous   h. laziness, drowsiness
___9. pernicious   i. querulous, irritable
___10. malice   j. explain, interpret

Words in context in *Othello*

Iago continues to nourish Othello's jealousy. He seemingly cautions Othello about being overly suspicious by saying that a mere friendly kiss or even an innocent lengthy embrace may not be wrong if the actions are performed without any adulterous intentions. In that case, the actions would be a mere "**venial** slip," a forgivable or trivial offense. Of course, such remarks only inflame Othello. Iago further fuels Othello's jealousy by reminding the general of the handkerchief. The ensign then says that Cassio has told him that he made love with Desdemona. This lie stokes Othello's fury to such feverish heights that the general goes into convulsions and collapses into unconsciousness.

Cassio then enters and sees the fallen Othello. He tells Iago to rub the general's temples, but Iago says that "the **lethargy** must have his quiet course." "**Lethargy**" currently means "sluggishness or drowsiness," but Shakespeare uses the word to have the stronger meaning of "coma." Iago thus tells Cassio to leave Othello alone until he comes out of the coma by himself. As Othello stirs, Iago tells Cassio to leave and come back later when Othello is gone. Iago then tells Othello that Cassio will come soon so that Othello should hide himself while Iago gets Cassio to talk about his affair with Desdemona. No sooner does Othello leave to his place of concealed observance, then Iago lets us know that Othello's

> ...jealousy must **construe**
> Poor Cassio's smiles, gestures, and light behavior
> Quite in the wrong.

Iago greets Cassio and gets him to talk about Bianca, a prostitute who loves Cassio. Othello **construes** or interprets Cassio's bantering remarks, light-hearted laughter, and disrespectful attitude toward Bianca as having to do with Desdemona. Bianca then arrives and presents Othello's hand-kerchief to Cassio. Iago has utterly convinced Othello that Desdemona and Cassio are lovers. When the general and his ensign are alone, Othello rages about how he will kill Desdemona. Iago suggests strangling her in her bed; Othello readily agrees.

Desdemona then brings an emissary who has come from Venice to Cyprus to convey a message to Othello. Othello strikes Desdemona in the presence of this Venetian official. When Othello and Desdemona depart, the astonished Venetian asks Iago about Othello's behavior. Iago answers,

> I may not breathe my **censure**
> What he may be.

The cunning Iago says that he can not speak with **censure** or disapproval and harsh criticism about his general, all the while implying that Othello has done and will do much worse.

Othello follows this violent display towards Desdemona with abusive words to her in private, accusing her of infidelity. Desdemona seeks consolation from Emilia and Iago. Iago assures her that oppressive state business accounts for Othello's mood and behavior.

Iago then meets Roderigo. The latter angrily accuses Iago of keeping the jewels that he was supposed to have given to Desdemona so that Roderigo could gain access to her. Roderigo says he will go to Desdemona and demand his presents back or, if finding that she never received them, take revenge on Iago. Once again, Iago successfully manipulates Roderigo by convincing this foolish man that he must immediately kill Cassio if he hopes to win Desdemona. Only such an incident will keep Othello and Desdemona in Cyprus; otherwise, lies Iago, Othello and Desdemona will leave to a distant part of Africa according to the commands delivered by the emissaries from Venice.

We then see the innocent Desdemona ask Emilia if she thinks there are actually women who commit adultery. Of course says her more worldly friend. Emilia explains that if wives are untrue it is because the husbands cheat on their wives even as these men "break out in **peevish** jealousies" and abuse their spouses. The deceived husbands only get what they deserve. Desdemona, herself a victim of **peevish** or ill-tempered jealousy, nevertheless yearns only to be true to her beloved Othello and to have her love reciprocated. She says good night to Emilia and sadly retires to bed.

Late that night Iago and Roderigo lay in wait to kill Cassio. Iago steps back a bit to let Roderigo do the actual murder, assuring him that he will come to his assistance if necessary. Iago then ponders how he will profit no matter who gets killed. Cassio's death will quelch the possibility that Othello will ever discover the truth from his former officer. If Roderigo dies, then Iago will not have Rodergio call him "to a **restitution**" or restoration of the precious jewels and gold that he cheated him out of. Roderigo then ambushes Cassio, but Cassio wounds his attacker. At this point, Iago jumps in and stabs Cassio in the leg. Cassio's scream attracts two officials. Iago then makes himself known to them (Cassio does not know that Iago maimed him). When Cassio points out his wounded attacker, Iago stabs Roderigo.

In the poignant scene that follows, Othello enters Desdemona's bedroom. Contemplating the sleeping Desdemona—the most precious love of his life—Othello steels every fiber of his being to carry through his resolve to kill her. He smothers her with a pillow. Emilia enters and Othello confesses himself the killer. To Emilia's astonishment, Othello says Desdemona committed adultery with Cassio and that it was Iago who first told him of it. Emilia says that if her husband said that then he is a liar and "may his **pernicious** soul rot." Emilia uses "pernicious" in an old sense of "evil, wicked" rather than in its modern sense of "harmful, injurious." She screams for help, and the governor of Cyprus, the Venetian emissary, and Iago enter.

Emilia confronts Iago and he admits what he told Othello. Othello adds that Desdemona gave his gift of a handkerchief to Cassio to reward Cassio's '**amorous** works" or lovemaking. As Iago tries to stop her, Emilia discloses that her husband had begged her to steal the handkerchief so that when she found it by accident, she gave it to him. Iago then fatally stabs her in the back and flees. Officers quickly capture and return with Iago, who has partially confessed his villainy. They also find a letter on the slain Roderigo that describes the plot to kill Cassio. Now fully conscious of the horror of his condition, Othello says,

> I pray you in your letters
> When you shall these unlucky deeds relate
> Speak of me as I am; nothing **extenuate**,
> Nor set down aught in **malice**. Then must you speak
> Of one that loved not wisely, but too well....

The noble general asks that the witnesses of these events do not **extenuate** or lessen the seriousness of his actions but also do not relate his story with **malice** or ill will. Othello then slays himself and falls next to Desdemona on their bridal and death bed.

REVIEW EXERCISE
Select the definition closest in meaning.

1. dilatory   (a) eager (b) bald (c) tardy (d) having much hair
2. bestial   (a) kind (b) intelligent (c) brutish (d) heroic
3. castigate   (a) praise (b) punish (c) help (d) isolate
4. alacrity   (a) style (b) quickness (c) dullness (d) loudness
5. mountebank   (a) genius (b) priest (c) swindler (d) baby
6. descry   (a) discover (b) grieve (c) ignore (d) laugh
7. lascivious   (a) skillful (b) happy (c) sad (d) lustful
8. egregious   (a) outstandingly bad (b) cold (c) hot (d) angry
9. obsequious   (a) proud (b) clever (c) servile (d) selfish
10. overt   (a) unconcealed (b) secret (c) passive (d) exact
11. construe   (a) sleep (b) interpret (c) escape (d) contradict
12. venial   (a) crucial (b) delicious (c) guilty (d) pardonable
13. extenuate   (a) lessen the seriousness (b) go (c) lie (d) cry
14. filch   (a) steal (b) pretend (c) lose (d) fly
15. inordinate   (a) excessive (b) small (c) orderly (d) dirty
16. ruminate   (a) meditate (b) cough (c) travel (d) dig a grave
17. inference   (a) conclusion (b) lie (c) enemy (d) blessing
18. iniquity   (a) reward (b) dirt (c) knowledge (d) wickedness
19. conjure   (a) summon by a spell (b) obey (c) laugh (d) cry
20. peevish   (a) cheerful (b) rude (c) irritable (d) unconcerned
21. tranquil   (a) uncertain (b) excited (c) hateful (d) peaceful
22. discern   (a) swallow (b) chew (c) perceive (d) worry
23. censure   (a) increase (b) praise (c) forget (d) blame
24. amorous   (a) spiteful (b) powerful (c) silly (d) loving
25. malice   (a) comfort (b) ill will (c) magic (d) loyalty
26. lethargy   (a) equality (b) vitality (c) pain (d) drowsiness
27. pernicious   (a) soothing (b) polite (c) useful (d) harmful
28. restitution   (a) crime (b) compensation (c) loss (d) law
29. surmise   (a) shock (b) guess (c) doubt (d) grip
30. politic   (a) stupid (b) organized (c) prudent (d) thin

6. King Lear

opulent	servile
propinquity	filial
wrath	equity
miscreant	defile
infirmity	wanton
peruse	ordinance
diligence	ample
carp	repose
epicure	simper
dissuade	reciprocal
halcyon	exasperate
antipathy	ebb
superfluous	patrimony
incense	heinous
rotundity	semblance

Learn these words from *King Lear*: Set I

1. *opulent* (OP yuh lunt) adj. wealthy or rich; abundant, plentiful, luxurious, lavish
The opulence of the Indian temple astounded us with its vast marble pillars and floors, magnificent sculptures ornamented with an abundance of precious jewels, and its breathtakingly beautiful lakes and gardens. In F. Scott Fitzgerald's *The Great Gatsby,* the wealthy Jay Gatsby throws extravagant parties, impressing everyone with his opulent home.

2. *propinquity* (pro PING kwih tee) n. nearness in time, place, or relationship; proximity; kinship
The phrase "he married the girl next door" shows that propinquity fosters love. The ties of propinquity transformed into knots of contention as the relatives battled over the inheritance of their ancestor's estate.

3. *wrath* (RATH) n. fierce anger, rage, indignation, ire
John Steinbeck took the title of his novel *The Grapes of Wrath* (1939) from these lines of the *Battle Hymn of the Republic*:

> Mine eyes have seen the glory of the coming of the Lord,
> He is trampling out the vintage where the grapes of wrath are stored.

The novel shows a family leaving Oklahoma during the Great Depression for a better life in California, only to experience in this land of grapes disillusion and bitter wrath.

4. *miscreant* (MISS cree unt) n. & adj. villain, evildoer; villainous
"Miscreant" derives from Middle English *miscreaunt* ("unbelieving"). In the Middle Ages, the Catholic Church viewed those who did not believe in its doctrines as unbelievers or infidels. Since unbelievers were considered evil, the word came to mean "villainous." By Shakespeare's time, the word could be used in its religious sense or in general to mean an evil scoundrel. Today, we consider terrorists and traitors miscreants. We detest miscreant providers of health care who knowingly perform needless surgery and provide harmful drugs for their own profit and their patients' detriment.

5. *infirmity* (in FUR mih tee) n. physical weakness, illness, character flaw or defect
The army refused to accept volunteers who had infirmities that would make them unfit on the battlefield. As we age, we may avoid becoming infirm or feeble if we exercise regularly and eat nutritiously. Of course, an infirmity of willpower to maintain proper exercise and diet will most likely hasten physical infirmity.

6. *peruse* (puh ROOZ) v. read carefully
 I cannot advise you to accept the offer until I peruse the documents. The judges in the literary contest gave an attentive reading or perusal to every entry. Shakespeare's contemporary, the English philosopher and statesman Francis Bacon (1561-1626), wrote, "Some books are to be tasted, others to be swallowed, and some few to be chewed and digested." In other words, some books are to be skimmed, others read, and a few perused.

7. *diligence* (DIL ih juns—rhymes with "intelligence") n. careful, constant, and persistent effort or work; assiduousness
Thomas Alva Edison's saying "genius is one per cent inspiration and ninety-nine per cent perspiration" means that creative output stems mainly from diligence. Outstanding students must be diligent as well as intelligent.

8. *carp* (KARP) v. unreasonably find fault over petty or minor concerns; complain, nitpick
Good, constructive critics help correct significant faults; narrow-minded, carping critics nitpick over matters of little or no importance. Teenagers sometimes feel that their parents continually carp over the most absurd issues.

9. *epicure* (EP ih kewr—rhymes with secure) n. person with refined taste for food and drink; connoisseur of fine dining, gourmet
"Epicure" comes from the Greek philosopher Epicurus (341-270 B.C.) who taught that pleasure was the highest good. Likewise, from him comes the word "epicurean" (ep ih kew REE un), as a noun meaning the same as "epicure"; as an adjective, "epicurean"—in addition to describing an epicure or epicurean—sometimes also describes one devoted to sensuous pleasure and a life of luxury. Actually, Epicurus himself advocated a life of simple moderation to maintain a peaceful mind and healthy

body. Shakespeare in *King Lear* uses the related form "epicurism" to mean "overindulgence in food and drink, riotous living." No epicure or expert in fine taste and dining would eat like a pig.

10. ***dissuade*** (dih SWAYD) v. persuade or advise not to do something
I would dissuade anyone from signing a contract before perusing or reading it carefully.

Working With Words

Complete the following sentences by using each of the following words only once: opulent, propinquity, wrath, miscreant, infirmity, peruse, diligence, carp, epicure, dissuade.

1. Judy's boyfriend made sure he got her home on time because he feared the _____ of her father.

2. You must _____ this essay with all your powers of concentration since it is extremely subtle, complex and, ultimately, richly rewarding.

3. I wish my teacher would sometimes praise my efforts rather than always _____ at my work.

4. My parents tried to _____ me from becoming an actor because they feared I would not be able to earn a living.

5. Our country home is in close _____ to a lake where we fish and swim.

6. In his American literary classic *Walden* (1854), Henry David Thoreau tells us that "most of the luxuries, and many of the so-called comforts of life, are not only not indispensable, but positive hindrances to the elevation of mankind." Thoreau opposes an _____ lifestyle and urges us to simplify our lives.

7. My grandfather's growing weakness or _____ eventually forced him to retire.

8. The _____ would dine only at the finest restaurants.

9. Would-be geniuses should know that inspiration comes not to those who idly wait for it but to those who work with _____; to paraphrase Edison, inspiration is the product of perspiration.

10. A plagiarist is a _____ who uses ideas or writings of another and presents them as his own.

Match the word on the left with its definition.

___1. infirmity	a. proximity, nearness, kinship
___2. dissuade	b. persistent effort
___3. opulent	c. evildoer
___4. peruse	d. advise not to do something
___5. carp	e. expert judge of fine dining
___6. propinquity	f. weakness
___7. miscreant	g. read carefully
___8. wrath	h. nitpick, complain
___9. epicure	i. wealthy, luxurious
___10. diligence	j. anger

Words in context of *King Lear*

Shakespeare sets *King Lear* in a mythic past before Christianity came to Britain. Long accustomed to imperious rule, the aged Lear (over eighty years old) decides to retire and divide his kingdom among his three daughters. His egotism blinds him to truth. When his youngest daughter fails to flatter his vanity, King Lear's rash act initiates a cataclysmic flood of suffering that pours on his old but foolish head.

Before formally dividing Britain into thirds among his daughters, King Lear in an elaborate palace ceremony asks them to tell which one loves him the most. The two eldest, Goneril and Regan, falsely flatter him and each receives her intended portion. He then asks his youngest and favorite daughter, Cordelia, what she can say to get "a third more **opulent** than her sisters." Disgusted by the deceitfully gushing words of her sisters, Cordelia—who truly loves her father but also shares his headstrong-ness—refuses to play along and answers, "Nothing, my lord." Prodded to say something more by Lear who truly wants to give her the most **opulent** or rich portion of his kingdom, Cordelia answers plainly and simply that she loves him according to the natural duty that binds a child to its parent, no more and no less. Enraged at her defiant resistance to stroke his ego, Lear proclaims,

> Here I disclaim all my paternal care,
> **Propinquity** and property of blood,

and dismisses her from his heart and kingdom. He severs his **propinquity** or kinship with her; he disinherits and disowns her. Lear's loyal councilor Kent jumps in to defend Cordelia, but the king immediately cuts him off, telling him not to come "between the dragon and his **wrath**". When Kent proceeds bluntly to tell Lear that he is a mad old man who has acted fool-ishly to his loving daughter Cordelia, the councilor only heightens the king's **wrath** or fierce anger. Lear calls him a **miscreant** or villain and tells him to leave the kingdom within ten days on pain of death.

King Lear then tells Cordelia's suitors that he disinherited her. One suitor leaves; the other, the King of France, loves her for herself and not her possessions. The French king declares that "she is herself a dowry."

After the court is dismissed and Cordelia leaves for France with her future husband, Goneril and Regan discuss King Lear's rash actions. Even they, who have no love for their sister, admit that their father showed extremely poor judgment toward Cordelia and Kent. As Regan says, "'Tis the **infirmity** of his age; yet he hath ever but slenderly known himself." Lear's foolish behavior is an **infirmity** or weakness of old age, what we might call senility. Nonetheless, Regan states that even when he was younger King Lear had little self-knowledge.

In the next scene, Edmund, illegitimate son of Lear's loyal nobleman Gloucester, plots against his older and legitimate brother Edgar. Gloucester comes upon Edmund who attempts to hide a letter. When Gloucester asks him about it, Edmund says that he has **perused** or read it and not found it fit for his father's inspection. This answer whets Gloucester's desire to see the letter; he demands it of Edmund. With feigned reluctancy, Edmund hands his father the letter. Actually, Edmund forged the letter in Edgar's handwriting. The contents suggest that Edmund should conspire with Edgar to murder their father and then divide his possessions between them. Edmund then pretends to soothe his father's wrath by saying that Edgar probably wrote the letter merely to test Edmund's love for Gloucester. Edmund explains that he will seek Edgar to discover the true situation. When Edmund meets his brother, he says that Gloucester is enraged with Edgar and that Edgar should stay away from their father until his wrath subsides.

Meanwhile, King Lear has gone to stay at the palace of Goneril and her husband Albany. Kent, ever loyal to Lear, has disguised himself so that he can remain in the kingdom and watch over his king. Kent comes incognito to Lear and asks to serve him. When Lear asks what are his qualifications, Kent replies that "the best of me is **diligence**" or careful, persistent effort. Goneril's steward Oswald, the manager of her house-hold, comes to them and—on orders from Goneril—treats the king with disrespect. Kent kicks Oswald off his feet and Lear rewards his former councilor by hiring him.

Lear's fool or court jester enters at this point. He, too, remains loyal to Lear but because of his special status as comic entertainer he can crit-icize Lear with impunity. The fool constantly alludes to Lear's mistake in divesting himself of power and dividing his kingdom, actually calling Lear the real fool. Lear tolerates criticism from his fool, but not from anyone else. When Goneril enters and tells her father that his one hundred attendants "do hourly **carp** and quarrel" and that their "**epicurism** and lust" make her palace seem like a tavern or house of prostitution, Lear rages. Although he has given away his power, he still expects to be treat-ed with the dignity due a king and will not suffer anyone denouncing his men for their **carping** or complaining and for their **epicurism** or pursuit of pleasure (more like "riotous behavior" as the word is used by Goneril). He curses her and exclaims,

> How sharper than a serpent's tooth it is
> To have a thankless child!

No sooner does he express this sentiment then he learns that Goneril has dismissed fifty of his men. He determines to leave Goneril for his other daughter Regan. But first he sends Kent with a letter to Regan preparing her for his visit. Goneril also sends Oswald with a letter conspiring against Lear to her sister Regan.

Regan and her husband Cornwall are on their way to Gloucester's castle. As Edmund awaits them there, his brother Edgar enters. Edmund says that Edgar must flee for his life before his father's men capture him. As Edgar leaves, Edmund wounds himself in the arm with his own sword. Edmund then explains to Gloucester that Edgar had come with the intent to persuade him to kill their father, but when Edmund "**dissuaded** him from his intent," Edgar had stabbed his brother. Gloucester accepts the story that Edgar came to murder him and Edmund tried to **dissuade** or persuade him not to. Regan and Cornwall then arrive at Gloucester's castle.

Learn these words from *King Lear*: Set II

1. *halcyon* (HAL see un) adj. peaceful, calm, pleasant, happy, tranquil
"Halcyon" comes from the Greek *halkyon* for the bird the kingfisher. According to a Greek myth, the kingfisher laid her eggs in a nest on the sea during which time the waters remained magically calm and peaceful. This period of tranquillity became known as the "halcyon days." We often remember the halcyon days of our youth as the most happy and carefree time of our lives.

2. *antipathy* (an TIP uh thee—rhymes with "sympathy") n. strong dislike, aversion
Mathematicians, who love their subject, cannot understand why so many people have an antipathy to mathematics.

3. *superfluous* (soo PUR floo us) adj. more than is needed or wanted; unnecessary, extra, surplus
We have already discussed the plan and made our decision; anything you now say will have no effect and be merely superfluous. "The paralysis of analysis" refers to a superfluity (soo pur FLOO ih tee) or excess and over-abundance of the talk and thought that inhibits action. A good synonym for "superfluity" is "plethora" (PLETH uh ruh). When I bumped into the taxi in front of me, the cabdriver showered me with a superfluity or plethora of abusive verbal expressions.

4. *incense* (in SENS) v. make very angry, enrage, infuriate
In *Travels with Charley* John Steinbeck, American author of *The Grapes of Wrath* and winner of the Nobel Prize, tells how he became incensed with racial injustice and prejudice when touring the South in the early 1960's. Cordelia's refusal to flatter her father, King Lear, incenses him. The verb "incense" and the noun "incense" (IN sens), which means "substance burned to produce a fragrant odor or its smoke," both derive from Latin "incendere" ("set on fire"). Thus, we light incense with a flame and can be inflamed or incensed in a heated argument.

5. *rotundity* (roh TUN dih tee) n. roundness, plumpness
Champion athletes vary in physique from the leanness of marathon runners to the rotundity of sumo wrestlers. Stout or rotund (roh TUND) William Howard Taft was our heaviest President (1909-1913), packing over three hundred pounds on his six-foot frame.

6. *servile* (SUR vul) n. slavishly submissive
Our boss appreciates constructive criticism but has an antipathy for insincere, servile flattery; he desires dedication, not servility (sur VIL uh tee).

7. *filial* (FIL ee ul) adj. pertaining to a son or daughter
In many societies it is a filial obligation for children to take care of their elderly parents.

8. *equity* (EK wih tee) n. justice, fairness; the value of a property or business after subtracting the amount owed on it
Robin Hood became an outlaw because the rule of the Sheriff of Nottingham was without equity. We believed the real estate agent when she told us how much the equity in our home was since she had a reputation for honest and equitable (EK wih tuh bul) business transactions. Justice is often pictured as a blindfolded woman holding scales to illustrate that legal decisions should be equitable or impartial and fair.

9. *defile* (dih FYL) v. make filthy, dirty, impure, or unclean; pollute, corrupt, dishonor, profane, desecrate
Our leader would not defile his reputation for equity and honesty by accepting campaign money having its origin in drugs and prostitution; he remained as undefiled in a community festering with corruption as a lotus blossom in a mud pond.

Working With Words

Complete the following sentences by using each of the following words only once: halcyon, antipathy, superfluous, incense, rotundity, servile, filial, equity, defile.

1. Do not _____ the dog by teasing it.

2. We associate a white beard, jollity, and _____ with Santa Claus.

3. When asked if he resented his wife's attention to her widowed mother, the husband replied that he respected, admired, and loved his wife all the more for her _____ care.

4. Be proud and not submissive; _____ behavior gets no respect.

5. Our peaceful, happy, _____ life ended with the outbreak of war.

6. Since the weather forecast said clear and sunny, we decided that umbrellas and raincoats would be _____ for our trip.

7. I have an _____ for cats but love dogs.

8. Only warped individuals would _____ a house of worship.

9. _____ demands that we listen carefully to both sides of an argument.

Vocabulary Power Through Shakespeare

Match the word on the left with its definition.

____1. halcyon   a. justice, fairness
____2. filial   b. roundness
____3. defile   c. extra, unnecessary
____4. servile   d. tranquil, calm, peaceful
____5. equity   e. slavishly submissive
____6. incense   f. aversion, strong dislike
____7. rotundity   g. infuriate
____8. superfluous   h. make filthy, corrupt, pollute
____9. antipathy   i. pertaining to a son or daughter

Words in context of *King Lear*

O
utside the castle, Kent and Oswald meet. Kent, hating Oswald for his insolence to Lear, attacks him. Cornwall, Regan, and Gloucester come to separate them. When Cornwall asks Kent why he is angry with Oswald, Kent pours a torrent of abuse on Oswald and says that Goneril's steward is one of those slavishly attentive servants who

> ...turn their **halcyon** beaks
> With every gale and vary of their masters,
> Knowing nought, like dogs, but following.

Today "**halcyon**" means "calm," but Kent uses the word in its literal meaning since "**halcyon**" is another name for the bird known as the king-fisher. It was believed that a dead kingfisher hung by the neck would turn in whatever direction the winds would vary. Just so Kent implies that Oswald mindlessly and obsequiously follows Goneril. Kent says that no two opposites "hold more **antipathy**" or strong dislike for each other than he and Oswald. When Oswald calmly tells Cornwall that he never offend-ed Kent, Cornwall takes Oswald's side and puts Kent in the stocks, a wooden frame that locks one's limbs so one is confined for a period to public humiliation.

When Lear arrives at Gloucester's castle, Cornwall and Regan release Kent from the stocks. Lear then complains of his treatment by Goneril to Regan. However, Goneril soon joins them at the castle and the two sisters unite against Lear. The sisters tell their father that he does not need a hun-dred men, not fifty, not twenty-five, not even one. Humiliated, distraught, and enraged, Lear exclaims,

> O, reason not the need! Our basest beggars
> Are in the poorest thing **superfluous**.

He says that even the poorest beggars have something that is **superfluous** or more than is absolutely needed. If you do not grant a man more than his most basic needs, then his life is worth no more than a beast's. On the verge of madness from the savage treatment by his daughters, Lear rush-es out from the castle accompanied by his fool. A dreadful storm begins to rage. Regan rationalizes that Lear's attendants may **incense** or inflame him to cause his daughters trouble. Therefore, Regan and Cornwall order Gloucester to lock his castle gates so that Lear cannot return for shelter .

The blasting wind and drenching rain accompanied by thunder and lightning mirror the chaos of Lear's suffering soul. Shelterless on the open wasteland or heath, Lear invokes the storm to "strike flat the thick **rotundity** o' the world," to crushingly flatten the **rotundity** or roundess of our planet. He calls himself a slave to the storm and forces of nature, nothing more than a "poor, infirm, weak, and despised old man." He then says that the rain, wind, thunder and lightening are "**servile** ministers" or slavish servants of nature that join forces with his daughters against him.

Back at the castle, Gloucester confides to Edmund that a rift grows between Albany and Cornwall. He also tells his son that French troops have landed in Britain to avenge Lear's injuries. Always loyal to Lear, Gloucester says that they must support the king. He adds that he will go to seek Lear in the storm and secretly help him.

By this time Kent has found Lear and the fool on the heath. Lear tells them that he is not concerned about his physical suffering. The tempest in his mind—caused by **filial** ingratitude or his children's thanklessness—so torments him that he cares not about the raging storm on the heath. Gloucester's son Edgar, disguised as a crazy beggar, then joins Lear's group. The once mighty and imperious Lear can now empathize with this homeless madman. In fact, his confrontation with Edgar results in Lear— already unbalanced by his sufferings—completely losing his mind. At this point Gloucester joins them on the heath. He does not recognize who Kent or Edgar really are. Gloucester then brings Kent, Edgar, and Lear to a farmhouse where there is food.

Here Lear holds a mock trial. He makes Edgar a judge and then makes the fool one also, referring to the fool as Edgar's "yoke-fellow of **equity**" or partner in justice. As the mad king, the seemingly mad beggar, and the fool hold crazy court to examine Goneril and Regan (who of course are not there), Gloucester tells Kent that there is a plot to kill Lear and that Kent must immediatley take the king for refuge to the city of Dover. When the others leave Edgar alone, Edgar says that he will reveal his true identity when he can prove his innocence against the falsehoods that now **defile** or dishonor him.

When Gloucester went to help Lear, Edmund betrayed his father to Cornwall. Gloucester is captured and brought back to his castle. Regan and Cornwall call him traitor. Regan yanks hairs from Gloucester's beard, and then Cornwall kicks out his eyes. In the process, a servant, revolted by the cruelty, draws his sword to stop Cornwall. Cornwall kills him, but not before receiving a wound from which he soon dies. As Regan orders Gloucester thrust out the gates, she says that Edmund informed about his treasons. Physically blinded, Gloucester now sees he has wronged his son Edgar.

Learn these words from *King Lear*: Set III

1. ***wanton*** (WON tun) adj. senseless and cruel; irresponsible; immoral; excessive; sexually unrestrained
The wanton slaughter of buffalo herds by U. S. citizens in the nineteenth century deprived many Native Americans of one of their main resources for survival. We hated the emperor for his wanton acts of cruelty. The Wife of Bath from Chaucer's *The Canterbury Tales*, the legendary Don Juan, and the real-life Casanova are wanton figures famed for their sexual adventures.

2. ***ordinance*** (OR din uns) n. authoritative command, order, law, or regulation, especially by a city government; decree
During the drought, the city issued an ordinance that prohibited homeowners from watering their lawns.

3. ***ample*** (AM pul) adj. large; abundant; adequate, sufficient
The rotund sumo wrestler was of ample proportions. We amply equipped our gymnasium with exercise devices to fit everyone's needs. I can blame no one but myself for losing my investment since I had ample warning that the stock I purchased was risky and unsound. The teacher told the class to amplify or develop and strengthen their writing with interesting details and convincing logic. Microphones amplify sound.

4. ***repose*** (rih POHZ) n. & v. rest
Harassed at the office and at home, Mr. Smith dreamed of escaping to a tropical island for some repose. She painted a romantic country scene where sweethearts reposed in their lovers' laps. A repository (rih POZ ih tor ee) is a place where we rest or store things for safekeeping; for example, a pharmacy is a repository for drugs, and a library is a repository for books.

5. ***simper*** (SIM pur) n. & v. smile, smirk
A simper is a silly, affected, or self-conscious smile. When our guest—a famous screen star—appeared before the class, the students first reacted with simpers and giggles. My friend advised me to ask intelligent questions, appear serious, and not simper during my job interview.

6. *reciprocal* (rih SIP ruh ul) adj. given or shown in return; affecting each in the same way; mutual
The reciprocal trade treaty between the two countries would strengthen both their economies. "If you scratch my back, I'll scratch yours" means that if you do me a favor I will reciprocate and do you a favor. According to the witty twentieth-century English writer Cyril Connolly, "The particular charm of marriage is the duologue, the permanent conversation between two people who talk over everything and everyone till death breaks the record. It is this back-chat which, in the long run, makes a reciprocal equality more intoxicating than any form of servitude or domination."

7. *exasperate* (ig ZAS puh rayt) v. intensely irritate or annoy, vex
Foolish talk exasperates the listener. The lecturer's boring narration caused audience exasperation.

8. *ebb* (EB) n. & v. flow of a tide as the water returns to the sea; decline, wane
The strength of the old fighter ebbed in the late rounds under a barrage of blows from his youthful opponent. The advent of democracy marked the ebb of the aristocracy.

9. *patrimony* (PAH truh mo nee) n. inheritance from father or ancestors; heritage, legacy
If "patrimony" is "inheritance from one's father," how come "matrimony" isn't "inheritance from one's mother"? Because their father was a billionaire, the children anticipated an ample—indeed, superfluously opulent—patrimony. The billionaire's death ignited sibling rivalry over the patrimonial (pah truh MO nee ul) wealth. We regard freedom as our patrimony since our fathers died defending it.

10. *heinous* (HAY nus) adj. hatefully bad or shockingly evil, atrocious
September 11, 2001 will be seared in our memory for the heinous attack on the World Trade Center.

11. *semblance* (SEM bluns) n. outward or superficial appearance; resemblance, likeness, guise
Artificial plants decorated her house, false friends with their simpering and servile smiles composed her society, and insincere words filled her prayers—all semblances of a life that was merely a pretense.

Working With Words

Complete the following sentences by using each of the following words only once: wanton, ordinance, ample, repose, simper, reciprocal, exasperate, ebb, patrimony, heinous, semblance.

1. The frenzied workaholic found lasting _____ in his cemetery plot.

2. We looked for a house with _____ space for our five children and two Saint Bernards.

3. The judge dismissed her speeding ticket with only a warning since it was the first time she had ever violated a traffic _____.

4. When my father died, he left me an ample _____ of stocks and real estate.

5. While mowing the lawn during an extremely hot and humid day, I felt my energy _____.

6. When my brother mentioned his impossibly impractical plans for starting a business, I tried to restore him to some _____ of reality.

7. Don't just stand there and _____ like a fool; wipe that smirk off your face and answer my question.

8. President Franklin Delano Roosevelt referred to the _____ Japanese attack on Pearl Harbor on December 7, 1941, as "a date which will live in infamy [evil fame]."

9. I lent him money hoping he would give me _____ help when I needed it.

10. Speaking to someone who pays no attention to what I am saying tends to _____ me.

11. The soldiers' _____ killing of unarmed villagers shocked our moral sensibility.

Match the word on the left with its definition.

____1. simper   a. heritage
____2. repose   b. wane, decline
____3. semblance   c. smirk
____4. ordinance   d. vex, irritate, annoy
____5. ample   e. rest
____6. heinous   f. atrocious, evil, bad
____7. reciprocal   g. decree, regulation, law
____8. patrimony   h. guise, resemblance
____9. ebb   i. mutual
____10. exasperate   j. senseless and cruel; irresponsible
____11. wanton   k. large, abundant, sufficient

Words in context of *King Lear*

The sightless Gloucester wanders on the heath. He meditates on the upheavals of fortune:

> As flies to **wanton** boys, are we to the gods;
> They kill us for their sport.

Life squashes us with the same meaningless absurdity as when **wanton** or senselessly cruel boys kill bugs. Gloucester then meets Edgar who still maintains the disguise of a mad beggar. Gloucester pities the supposed beggar, hands him money, and wishes that the luxurious rich—who contemptuously disregard the **ordinance** or law of heaven and have no sympathy for the needy—would suffer adversity. Gloucester asks that he be taken to a cliff from which he can jump to end his misery.

While Edgar leads his father, Kent meets the French army camp near Dover. When Kent asks if Cordelia, now the Queen of France, expressed grief after she received letters about Lear's condition, an attendant of Cordelia replies,

> Ay, sir; she took them, read them in my presence;
> And now and then an **ample** tear trilled [trickled] down
> Her delicate cheek.

Cordelia's **ample** or large tears express grief for her father. Kent states that Lear will not see Cordelia because he burns with shame for the way he treated her. Kent then takes Cordelia's attendant to Lear.

Cordelia appears at the French camp and asks a doctor what can be done to restore her father's sanity. The doctor says that "our foster-nurse of nature is **repose**." In other words, the caring nurse of our nature is **repose** or rest which the doctor can induce through herbal medicine. Cordelia sends some men to bring Lear to her.

Meanwhile, Edgar has brought his father to what Gloucester believes is the edge of a high cliff. The blind nobleman falls forward to commit suicide. Assuming a different accent, Edgar then tells his father that he had seen him drop from a great height and that it is miraculous that he is not dead or seriously injured. Father and son then meet Lear whose voice Gloucester recognizes. The mad king, smarting from the cruel treatment of Goneril and Regan, erupts in a tirade against women. He rails at the

simpering or smiling lady who appears so virtuous and chaste but in reality is more promiscuous than animals in heat. Cordelia's men then find them but Lear runs off with his daughter's men in pursuit.

At this point Oswald appears and tries to kill Gloucester. Edgar intervenes and kills Oswald. He then searches Oswalds's pockets and finds a letter from Goneril addressed to Edmund which begins, "Let our **reciprocal** vows be remembered." Goneril refers to their **reciprocal** or mutual vows of love and asks Edmund to kill Albany so that she can marry Edmund.

By this time Cordelia's men have found Lear and bring him to their queen. Lear cannot at first believe that Cordelia is really before him. With tearful and loving words, Cordelia consoles him. As Cordelia takes her father for a walk, Kent enters and tells the queen's attendant that Cornwall has died and Edmund now leads Regan's forces.

As the British camp prepares to combat the French army, Edgar, still in disguise, delivers to Albany Goneril's love letter to Edmund. Edgar tells Albany to read it before fighting Cordelia's troops. If Albany wins the battle, Edgar says he will produce a champion that will prove by trial of combat the truth of the letter's contents.

After Edgar and Albany part, Edmund enters and speaks aloud his thoughts:

> To both these sisters [Goneril and Regan] have I sworn my love;
> Each jealous of the other....
> Which of them shall I take?
> Both? One? Or neither? Neither can be enjoyed
> If both remain alive: to take the widow [Cornwall has died]
> **Exasperates**, makes mad her sister Goneril.

As long as both sisters are alive, Edmund's choosing one will **exasperate** or extremely irritate and infuriate the other. He goes on to say that Albany, who always was sympathetic to Lear, plans to show mercy to Lear and Cordelia once the French are defeated. Edmund, however, will make sure that they receive no mercy.

The British win the battle, and Edmund captures Lear and Cordelia. As guards take them away, Lear tells Cordelia that in prison they will constantly comfort each other as the various political powers "**ebb** and flow"; in other words, their mutually supportive love will remain constant admist the **ebb** or decline and flow or rise of contending rulers. However, this consoling future vision will not materialize because Edmund has sent an officer to kill them once they reach prison.

Albany then reenters the British camp with Goneril and Regan. The two sisters jealously argue about Edmund. Regan must cut short her angry words, however, since she feels ill (she has been poisoned by Goneril). Regan then tells Edmund to take charge of her "soldiers, prisoners, **patrimony**" or inheritance and proclaims that he will be her husband.

As Regan gives commands to inaugurate the marriage ceremony, Albany takes charge. He arrests Edmund for **heinous** or evil treason. Albany announces that if no one comes to prove Edmund a traitor by trial of combat, then Albany himself will fight Edmund to the death. Edgar (still disguised but in a more noble fashion than previously) now enters, challenges Edmund, and mortally wounds him. Albany then shows Goneril her treasonous love letter. She runs off.

Edgar becomes more charitable to his dying brother and asks Edmund that they forgive each other. Edgar reveals his true identity and tells how he assumed the **semblance** or appearance of a mad beggar and took care of their father. Shortly before the trial by combat, Edgar had put on his armor and revealed himself to Gloucester. The excitement proved too much and Gloucester died.

A man next rushes in holding a bloody knife. He frantically exclaims that both Goneril and Regan are dead, the former by suicide with the bloody blade he now grasps, the latter poisoned by her sister. Edmund tries to make amends by telling Albany and Edgar to stop the officer that he had sent to kill Lear and Cordelia. Too late. Lear appears with the dead Cordelia in his arms. The king had managed to kill the officer who hanged Cordelia, but not in time to save her. King Lear takes a last look at his beloved daughter, thinks that he detects her breathing, and dies.

REVIEW EXERCISE
Select the definition closest in meaning.

1. infirmity (a) wisdom (b) anger (c) happiness (d) weakness
2. semblance (a) anxiety (b) resemblance (c) resentment (d) hope
3. antipathy (a) relationship (b) dislike (c) sympathy (d) love
4. defile (a) sharpen (b) make dull (c) pollute (d) aggravate
5. ample (a) sufficient (b) ugly (c) attractive (d) unpleasant
6. opulent (a) wealthy (b) absolute (c) clear sighted (d) unnatural
7. dissuade (a) advise against (b) clean up (c) make dirty (d) cut
8. servile (a) healthy (b) sad (c) submissive (d) dominant
9. ordinance (a) stadium (b) blessing (c) servant (d) regulation
10. equity (a) excitement (b) justice (c) hatred (d) precision
11. halcyon (a) stormy (b) natural (c) huge (d) peaceful
12. miscreant (a) old woman (b) bachelor (c) villain (d) hero
13. superfluous (a) extra (b) insufficient (c) powerful (d) weak
14. wanton (a) senseless and cruel (b) spicy (c) good (d) soft
15. wrath (a) anger (b) laughter (c) humor (d) sickness
16. peruse (a) crawl (b) wake up (c) become drowsy (d) read
17. incense (a) enrage (b) applaud (c) support (d) meditate
18. filial (a) empty (b) of a son or daughter (c) full (d) relaxed
19. heinous (a) clean (b) soiled (c) hard (d) shockingly evil
20. patrimony (a) marriage (b) relative (c) heritage (d) patriotism
21. propinquity (a) nearness (b) exclusiveness (c) ownership (d) favor
22. rotundity (a) scarcity (b) theft (c) unhappiness (d) roundness
23. ebb (a) scrape (b) rise (c) decline (d) light
24. repose (a) rest (b) excitement (c) shame (d) entertainment
25. epicure (a) expert of fine dining (b) critic (c) fool (d) leader
26. diligence (a) sloppy (b) lazy (c) unnatural (d) persistent effort
27. exasperate (a) tickle (b) irritate (c) soothe (d) forget
28. simper (a) smile (b) frown (c) laugh (d) control
29. reciprocal (a) unlikely (b) sudden (c) mutual (d) impossible
30. carp (a) praise (b) educate (c) complain (d) embrace

7. A Midsummer Night's Dream

wane	preposterous
pomp	derision
vexation	sojourn
lamentable	amiable
extempore	upbraid
entreat	enamor
progeny	loathe
dissension	visage
entice	amity
dank	seethe
flout	tedious
disdainful	premeditate
surfeit	audacious
prologue	epilogue
odious	reprehend

Learn these words from *A Midsummer Night's Dream*: Set I

1. *wane* (WAYN) v. decline in power, intensity, influence, importance; become gradually smaller or weaker; draw to an end or close
The moon wanes when it decreases in size and roundness as it passes from a full to a new moon. My interest in sports faded or waned after I graduated from college. Young bucks challenged the old stag for leadership of the herd as they sensed his waning powers. As the day wanes and the sun sinks into the horizon, the farm hands head back to their bunks. The noun "wane" means "a gradual decrease or decline."

2. *pomp* (POMP) n. showy, splendid or magnificent display; ostentation
Graduation ceremonies are a time for pomp and celebration. A pompous (POM pus) person tries to seem important by showing off in a way that is too dignified or pretentious. Displays of pomposity (pom POS ih tee) therefore appear ridiculous rather than dignified.

3. *vexation* (vek SAY shun) n. annoyance, irritation, trouble, distress
Our unmade beds, unwashed dishes, and undone chores contributed to our mother's vexation. The doctor said it would help to control my blood pressure if I did not let little things vex me. I find her whiny, screechy voice vexatious.

4. *lamentable* (luh MEN tuh bul) pitifully sorrowful, regrettably unfortunate, deplorable
After Paul worked two full-time jobs the whole summer to pay for college, we found it lamentable that he could not go but had to stay home and help support his family when his father suffered a stroke. "Lament" can be a verb as when we lament or grieve for friends who died in a plane crash; "lament" can also be a noun as when we heard the howling lament or mourning of the Seeing Eye dog for her recently deceased owner.

5. *extempore* (ik STEM puh ree) adj. & adv. without preparation, unrehearsed, off-hand, impromptu
When actors improvise or say their lines on the spur of the moment and not from memory, they speak extempore or impromptu (im PROMP too). The adjective "extemporaneous" (ik stem puh RAY nee us) means the same as "extempore" or "impromptu." Some professors give excellent extempore, extemporaneous, or impromptu lectures without any notes or

157

preparation. Often, a speech seems more natural and appealing when one delivers it extempore, impromptu, or extemporaneously.

6. ***entreat*** (en TREET) v. ask earnestly, beg, plead, implore
My children entreat me to let them stay up to see the late-night movie. My own parents would never bend their rules for me no matter how persuasive my entreaty or pleading request.

7. ***progeny*** (PRAHJ uh nee) n. children, offspring, descendants
My grandparents were fruitful and multiplied; their progeny includes eleven children and sixty-seven grandchildren. We honor our progenitor (proh JEN ih tur) or ancestor who first came to the United States.

8. ***dissension*** (dih SEN shun) n. disagreement, especially one that causes hostility within a group; quarrel, discord, strife
"Dissension" suggests a difference of opinion that fosters hostility. "Dissent" (dih SENT) may be a noun meaning "disagreement" or a verb meaning "disagree," not necessarily suggesting bad feeling. In other words, a teacher may encourage students to dissent from her opinion, but the dissent must be presented rationally and respectfully so as not to arouse angry and chaotic dissension.

9. ***entice*** (en TYS, rhymes with "precise") v. tempt, lure, attract, allure
I resisted the enticement of chocolate fudge cake and stuck to my diet. In Greek mythology, the beautiful singing of the Sirens from an island surrounded by rocks would entice sailors to their death. Therefore, a seductively beautiful woman who entices or lures men is called a siren. Samson yielded to the enticements of the siren Delilah.

10. ***dank*** (DANK) adj. unpleasantly damp
I ruined my books by storing them in a dank basement. We could imagine the misery of former prisoners when we visited the dank dungeon.

Working With Words

Complete the following sentences by using each of the following words only once: wane, pomp, vexation, lamentable, extempore, entreat, progeny, dissension, entice, dank.

1. My little brother would _____ me to let him ride my bicycle.

2. The _____ among the jury made it almost impossible to reach a verdict.

3. When I first saw my dreary, dark, and _____ apartment, my heart sank.

4. As the years passed in the simple and pleasant surroundings of the monastery, the former soldier's memories of slaughter and starvation began to _____ .

5. My radical politics, rebellious friends, and decision not to join his firm accounts for my conservative, strait-laced father's _____ with me.

6. Although she had never married or had children, the professor regarded the college as her family and the students as her intellectual _____ .

7. I find it _____ that an initial interest in exercise for health can turn into an obsessive competiveness that results in injuries from overexertion.

8. Some like the _____ and pagentry that comes with high office; others like to wield power quietly and unconspicuously away from the public spotlight.

9. Can I _____ you away from your present job by doubling your salary if you work for me?

10. Because the celebrity excelled at _____ remarks, interviewers knew he would always be a good guest even at a moment's notice.

Match the word on the left with its definition.

____1. lamentable   a. offspring
____2. wane   b. unrehearsed
____3. progeny   c. showy display
____4. dissension   d. unpleasantly damp
____5. entreat   e. tempt
____6. vexation   f. disagreement
____7. dank   g. plead
____8. extempore   h. become smaller or weaker
____9. entice   i. annoyance
____10. pomp   j. sorrowful

Words in context of *A Midsummer Night's Dream*

S et in mythical times in the city of Athens in ancient Greece, *A Midsummer Night's Dream* begins as Duke Theseus of Athens speaks to Hippolyta, Queen of the Amazons, of their forthcoming wedding:

> Now, fair Hippolyta, our nuptial hour
> Draws on apace; four happy days bring in
> Another moon—but O methinks, how slow
> This old moon **wanes**.

Theseus eagerly anticipates the upcoming wedding that will take place in four days with the coming of a new moon, but for a lover those four days until the old moon **wanes** or comes to an end drag slowly. He tells his director of entertainment to "stir up the Athenian youth to merriments....with **pomp** and revelling." While Theseus prepares for his wedding with **pomp** or magnificent displays and joyous amusements, a nobleman troubled by his daughter's refusal to marry the man he selected for her comes to the duke. The working out of this problem, an amateur play production for the royal wedding, and the enchantment of fairyland interweave in this magical, lighthearted comedy that culminates in a triple wedding.

The nobleman tells Theseus,

> Full of **vexation** come I, with complaint
> Against my child, my daughter Hermia.

The nobleman is full of **vexation** or greatly troubled because his daughter Hermia has fallen in love with Lysander and thus refuses to marry Demetrius, the father's choice. Theseus rules she must be obedient to her father's will. If in four days—the date of Theseus and Hippolyta's wedding—she will not marry Demetrius, then she must either die or become a nun and remain chaste in a monastery for the rest of her life.

Left alone, Lysander and Hermia discuss their plight. He comments that "the course of true love never did run smooth." He then suggests that they go to his aunt who lives some twenty miles away outside the power of Athenian law and there get married. They will meet the next night in the woods outside Athens and run away. Hermia passionately swears to join him. They then tell their friend Helena—whose heart Demetrius won before he fell in love with Hermia—of their plan. When Lysander and Hermia leave her, Helena says she will inform Demetrius, whom she still loves, of Hermia's flight.

The scene then shifts to Athenian workmen who prepare to produce a play for the duke's wedding. These goodhearted, simple, unsophisticated folk are well-meaning but deficient actors. They decide to perform a play which they call "the most **lamentable** comedy, and most cruel death of Pyramus and Thisbe." Of course, a **lamentable** or sorrowful comedy is a contradiction, but such matters do not bother their less than subtle theatrical minds. The play dramatizes the myth of the handsome youth Pyramus and his beautiful lover Thisbe. Their parents, whose homes are separated by a wall, prohibit their marriage. Through a chink in this wall, the young lovers communicate. One day, they decide to run away and meet that night at the tomb of a king. Thisbe arrives first but sees a lion by moonlight. She drops her cloak and flees. The lion, with mouth bloody from a recent kill, then mauls the garment. Pyramus arrives, sees the bloodstained cloak, concludes that Thisbe is dead, and kills himself with his sword. Thisbe returns, realizes what happened, and plunges her lover's sword into her heart. Peter Quince, a carpenter and the soundest in judgment of the workers, directs the play; Nick Bottom, a weaver and the most boisterously enthusiastic of the actors, plays Pyramus. Another actor, Snug, who will play the part of the lion, fears he may not learn his lines in time because he has trouble memorizing. Quince reassures him that he "may do it **extempore**, for it is nothing but roaring." Since a roar requires no preparation, Snug can do his part **extempore** or without rehearsal. Quince then says to the amateur cast,

> Here are your parts, and I am to **entreat** you, request you,
> and desire you, to con [learn] them by tomorrow night,
> and meet me in the palace wood, a mile without the town,
> by moonlight.

Quince **entreats** or implores his fellow workmen to learn their parts so they will be ready for rehearsal the next night.

In the same forest where the cast will rehearse and where the four Athenian lovers have gone, Oberon, king of the fairies, and Titania, queen of the fairies, accidentally meet. Titania had left Oberon to live by herself. No sooner do they meet than they begin a jealous quarrel. Titania says that nature's harmony has been disrupted by their constant fighting which causes epidemics, floods, failed crops, and unseasonable weather:

> And this same **progeny** of evils comes
> From our debate, from our **dissension**.

The **progeny** or offspring of their **dissension** or quarreling are the disruptions of nature that now plague the land. Oberon says they can end these evils if Titania would only give him a little boy to be his attendant. Titania refuses to let Oberon have this boy. She says that the boy's mother was a devotee of hers from India who died giving birth to him.

> And for her sake do I rear up her boy,
> And for her sake I will not part with him.

When Titania leaves, Oberon calls for Puck, a mischievous fairy in his service. He tells Puck that Cupid's arrow once missed its mark and landed on a flower making it a love potion. Place the juice of this flower on someone's sleeping eyelids and the person will fall madly in love with the first creature the individual sees upon waking. Oberon sends Puck to fetch this flower. The fairy king plans to use this potion on Titania and not remove its spell until he gets the Indian boy from her.

At this point Demetrius enters followed by Helena. Oberon makes himself invisible so that he can overhear their conversation. Demetrius tells Helena,

> Do I **entice** you? Do I speak you fair [speak kindly to you]?
> Or, rather, do I not in plainest truth
> Tell you I do not nor I cannot love you?

Demetrius says that he does not **entice** or lure her and does not love her. He further rebukes Helena by saying he will harm her if she follows him in the forest. After they depart and Puck returns with the flower, Oberon decides to help Helena by making Demetruis reciprocate her love. He tells Puck to put some of the love potion on the eyelids of a man whom Puck will recognize by the man's Athenian clothes. Oberon then finds Titania sleeping and anoints her eyes with the flower's juice.

By this time Lysander and Hermia have lost their way in the woods and decide to lie down and rest. For modesty's sake, Lysander separates himself a considerable distance from Hermia. Puck arrives, sees Lysander in his Athenian clothes, and notices "the maiden sleeping sound on the **dank** and dirty ground." Puck assumes that Hermia on the **dank** or damp ground is the despised maid forced to lie apart from the man she loves. Puck then squeezes drops from the magic flower on Lysander's eyelids and returns to the fairy king.

Learn these words from *A Midsummer Night's Dream:* Set II

1. *flout* (FLOWT, rhymes with "shout") v. scorn or mock
The defiant student expressed his contempt for authority when he flouted the formal dress code regulation by appearing in only his underwear. If you flout the warnings about excessive eating and alcoholic drinking, you may get gout (a painful inflammation of the joints, especially in the big toe).

2. *disdainful* (dis DAYN ful) adj. scornful and contemptuous
The arrogant prince treated his servants disdainfully. After he lost his money and health, the once disdainful egotist became quite humble and even compassionate. "Disdain" can be a noun meaning "contempt" or a verb meaning "show contempt or scorn, think unworthy of notice or response." In Aesop's fable of the lion and mouse, a lion grabs a mouse but disdains to kill it. Later when the lion becomes entangled in a hunter's net and the mouse sets him free by chewing through the rope, the lion's disdain changes to appreciation.

3. *surfeit* (SUR fit) n. excess or overindulgence, especially in food and drink
The wedding reception provided a surfeit of rich food and expensive champagne. The verb "surfeit" means "supply or feed to excess." The children surfeited on sweets at the birthday party; that evening they all had stomachaches.

4. *prologue* (PRO log) n. introduction
The prologue of *Romeo and Juliet* gives background information about the play and sketches the plot by telling how it will take the deaths of "a pair of star-crossed lovers" from feuding families to reconcile the households. When the infant Hercules grasped a deadly serpent in each fist and squeezed the life from them, the act was a prologue to his future heroic feats.

5. *odious* (OH dee us) adj. hateful, offensive, disgusting, repulsive, repugnant, abhorrent
After hearing the prophecy of three witches, the once valiantly noble Macbeth becomes an odious villain who kills—among others—his comrade, his king, and an innocent woman and her child.

6. **preposterous** (prih POS tur us) adj. ridiculous, obviously absurd, contrary to reason
Do you find it preposterous to have a pet rhinoceros? Do not take Mr. Abe Surd as your business partner; he talks rationally but will act preposterously.

7. **derision** (dih RIZH un, rhymes with "vision") n. ridicule, mockery
After his business venture failed, the merchant had to endure his rival's derision. When the ailing prisoner asked for a doctor, his cruel guards responded with derisive (dih RY siv) or mocking gestures. The massive thug laughed with contempt and derided his elderly, frail-looking victim when the old man warned him not to use violence; however, the supposed victim—a world famous judo master—had the last laugh.

8. **sojourn** (SOH jurn) n. temporary stay, visit & v. stay, visit, or reside temporarily
Every summer we sojourn in our cottage in Victoria, Canada. Life on this planet is a mere sojourn; we are all sojourners here during our brief stay.

Working With Words

Complete the following sentences by using each of the following words only once: flout, disdainful, surfeit, prologue, odious, preposterous, derision, sojourn.

1. One of the most famous introductions in literature is Chaucer's _____ to *The Canterbury Tales*.

2. We enjoyed our month's _____ in London before returning to our home in Nashville, Tennessee.

3. Whereas my older sister always wanted to obey the rules, my rebellious younger sister would continually _____ authority.

4. When the researcher advertised for subjects willing to participate in a study showing the effects of chocolate ice cream on memory, she had a _____ of applications.

5. The physically deformed and shockingly evil Richard III is one of Shakespeare's most _____ villains.

6. The spoiled, pampered princess thought no one worthy of her and snubbed her suitors with _____ contempt.

7. Our ancestors would have considered air travel, instantaneous worldwide communication, and transplants of vital organs _____ .

8. If someone would have predicated our modern achievements in transportation, communication, and medicine to our ancestors, they might have laughed in _____ .

Vocabulary Power Through Shakespeare

Match the word on the left with its definition.

___1. disdainful	a. scorn or mock
___2. prologue	b. introduction
___3. preposterous	c. ridiculous
___4. sojourn	d. excess
___5. odious	e. mockery
___6. surfeit	f. visit
___7. flout	g. contemptuous
___8. derision	h. hateful

Words in context of *A Midsummer Night's Dream*

Helena now finds her way to the sleeping Lysander. He awakes and declares his love for her. Helena thinks Lysander mocks her and says it's bad enough that Demetrius rejects her but now Lysander "must **flout** my insufficiency....in such **disdainful** manner me to woo." She feels that Lysander **flouts** or mocks her because she is insufficient in beauty and therefore he **disdainfully** or contemptuously woos her. As Helena runs away, Lysander says,

> She sees not Hermia. Hermia, sleep thou there,
> And never mayst thou come Lysander near.
> For, as a **surfeit** of the sweetest things
> The deepest loathing to the stomach brings...
> So thou, my **surfeit**...
> Of all be hated, but the most of me!

Just as a **surfeit** or excess of sweets becomes hateful to the stomach, so Hermia has become hateful to Lysander. He then pursues Helena. Hermia wakes from a nightmare to discover that she is alone. She determines to find Lysander.

In another part of the forest, the Athenian workmen meet to rehearse their play. Bottom says the women will be afraid when they see Pyramus kill himself. Bottom therefore suggests that they "write...a **prologue**...to say we will do no harm with our swords, and that Pyramus is not killed...and that I, Pyramus, am not Pyramus, but Bottom the weaver." While stating the ridiculously obvious, this **prologue** or introduction conveys the childlike naiveté of the actors. Bottom further illustrates his comic ineptitude when as Pyramus he recites his line, "Thisbe, the flowers of **odious** savors sweet," bungling what should be "odorous savors sweet" or sweet smells into **odious** or disgustingly repulsive smells.

Unknown to the actors, Puck has been observing their rehearsal. When Bottom temporarily departs from the other actors after saying some lines, the mischievous Puck transforms Bottom's head into that of an ass or donkey. As Bottom returns to his group, the others see his monstrous disfigurement and flee. Bottom then comes upon the sleeping Titania who wakes, looks upon him, and falls in love.

Meanwhile, Oberon has informed Puck that Puck put the love potion on the wrong man. Oberon begins to remedy the error by putting the love potion on the eyelids of a sleeping Demetrius. He tells Puck to bring

Helena here so that Demetrius will wake to love her. Puck, amused by the confusing events, says,

> Lord, what fools these mortals be...
> Then will two at once woo one...
> And those things do best please me
> That befall **preposterously**.

He is happiest observing life at its most **presposterous** or ridiculously absurd.

Helena then appears, still pursued by Lysander. Lysander protests that his love is sincere:

> Why should you think that I should woo in scorn?
> Scorn and **derision** never come in tears.

His tears prove a sincerity devoid of **derision** or mockery. The nearby Demetrius wakes up, sees Helena, and proclaims his love. Helena thinks they both mock her. Demetrius declares,

> Lysander, keep thy Hermia; I will none.
> If e'er I loved her, all that love is gone.
> My heart to her but as guest-wise **sojourned**,
> And now to Helen is it home returned,
> There to remain.

Demetrius states that his passion for Hermia was a mere **sojourn** or temporary visit and he now returns to stay with his true love Helena. Hermia then enters this scene. The four lovers create a scene of hilarious confusion and outrage. Lysander leaves followed by Demetrius who seeks him for a duel.

Oberon and Puck, unnoticed by the four mortals, have observed their meeting and departure. Oberon tells Puck to cloud the night sky and imitate the voices of Lysander and Demetrius so as to confuse these two men about each other's whereabouts; in this way they will be led astray and not find each other for a sword fight. Finally, Lysander and Demetrius grow weary and fall asleep, unaware that they lie near each other. Weary and unaware that they wander near Lysander and Demetrius, Helena and Hermia come near the men and also lie down and sleep. Puck then applies a magical antidote on Lysander's eyes to remove the spell of the love potion. When the mortals awake, Lysander will love Hermia and Demetrius will love Helena.

Learn these words from *A Midsummer Night's Dream*: Set III

1. *amiable* (A [pronounced like the letter "a"] mee uh bul) adj. friendly, good-natured, pleasant, cordial, congenial
Susannah's amiable personality wins her many friends. Do not fight with your brother but settle your differences amiably. Guard dogs like Doberman pinschers do not have reputations for amiability with strangers.

2. *upbraid* (up BRAYD) v. scold or criticize severely; reproach, reprimand
The coach upbraided us for playing sloppy basketball.

3. *enamor* (ih NAM ur) v. inflame or fill with love; charm, captivate
We knew we were in for a long evening since the speaker was enamored with his own voice. Passionate readers are enamored of books.

4. *loathe* (rhymes with "clothe" as in "I will clothe you in a mink coat")
v. dislike intensely, hate, detest
What do you do when you love someone who loathes you? The monster filled us with fear and loathing. Do not confuse "loathe" with "loath" (rhymes with "both") which means "reluctant, unwilling, averse." Although I was offered a generous salary, I am loath to work for a company whose products I loathe.

5. *visage* (VIZ ij) n. face, appearance, countenance
Perhaps the most famous visage in literature is that of Helen of Troy of which Christopher Marlowe (an English playwright and poet born the same year as Shakespeare) wrote: "Was this the face that launched a thousand ships..."

6. *amity* (AM ih tee) n. friendly or peaceful relations; friendship
The United Nations strives for amity among the nations of the world.

7. *seethe* (SEETH, rhymes with "breathe") v. be disturbed or agitated; boil
"Seethe" means "to bubble, foam, or boil" as when the surf seethes with foam or a boiling teakettle seethes. "Seethe" also means to boil in agitation or rage. As my father saw me parking his new sports car after return-

ing from a small collision, he seethed in anger. When I asked him if he was happy I did not get hurt, his seething temper erupted like a volcano.

8. *tedious* (TEE dee us) adj. tiresomely long or dull; boring, wearisome
The neglected housewife thought her life was one long tedious routine of doing the same chores over and over and over again. She tried to relieve her tedium or boredom and weariness by watching soap operas and reading romance novels.

9. *premeditate* (pree MED ih tayt) v. plan or think out in advance
Although the actor's response to the questions seemed impromptu, his answers were the product of lengthy premeditation earlier that day with publicity agents. The prosecuting attorney demonstrated that the defendant's slaying of his wife for infidelity was not an instantaneous passionate reaction but a predmeditated murder that he had planned for months. The professor would never consciously premeditate or plan in advance his classroom lectures so they always seemed natural and spontaneous; however, his lifetime of study might be considered an unconscious premeditation.

10. *audacious* (aw DAY shus) adj. bold, daring, reckless; shamelessly rude, disrespectful, or insolent
"Audacious" can mean "shamelessly disrespectful"; "audacious" can also mean "daring or bold" in either a reckless or a spirited and positive way. When David volunteered to fight Goliath, many thought David would be slain after his audacious or bold and daring decision to fight Goliath. During class a student corrected a faulty quotation of the teacher; the pompous instructor regarded the act as audacious or insolent, evidently believing that no one would have the audacity (aw DAS ih tee) or insolence to question his knowledge. Of course, the rest of the class admired their fellow student for her audacity or daring boldness to confront the teacher.

11. *epilogue* (EP uh log) n. concluding speech or poem spoken directly to an audience at end of a play; concluding part of a literary work
The prologue of the play introduced the background for the events that would follow, and the epilogue told the fate of the characters after the play's action had concluded. In the epilogue to her historical novel, the author explained to what extent she had either conformed to or imaginatively amplified and deviated from the recorded facts.

12. ***reprehend*** (rep rih HEND) find fault with; scold, blame, rebuke
The manager reprehended the night watchman for falling asleep. "Reprehend" commonly appears in its adjective form "reprehensible" (rep rih HEN suh bul) meaning "blameworthy." Because the sleeping night watchman was considered reprehensible for not preventing the recent thefts, he was fired.

Working With Words

Complete the following sentences by using each of the following words only once: amiable, upbraid, enamor, loathe, visage, amity, seethe, tedious, premeditate, audacious, epilogue, reprehend.

1. My roommate would _____ me for returning drunk in the middle of the night and waking him by slamming the door.

2. Although their countries had a long history of bitter conflict, the two foreign students in my university laboratory became close friends and maintained an _____ relationship for the rest of their lives.

3. In the _____ to his collection of scientific essays written over the last thirty years, the author describes important discoveries made after some of the essays were written.

4. The violinist performed so perfectly that not even the harshest and most severe critics could find anything to _____.

5. While my ex-wife cataloged my faults to my girlfriend, I began to _____ in anger.

6. The prosecutor showed beyond doubt that the victim's death was not an accident by proving that the accused did indeed _____ the murder.

7. If marching across the stage in the nude at your graduation ceremony is bold and reckless, would strolling through a nudist colony with your clothes on be considered equally _____ ?

8. Is it possible to love our enemies rather than _____ them?

9. The jagged scar, torn ear, and large canine teeth made his _____ terrifying.

10. After the Civil War, Abraham Lincoln sought to erase enmity or hatred between North and South and to restore _____ or friendly relations.

11. Fragrant incense, sparkling jewels, and rapturous music _____ my senses.

12. Dr. Samuel Johnson, author of a great eighteenth-century English dictionary, must have thought this task _____ because he wrote these lines after completing the work:

> And weary of his task, with wondering eyes,
> Saw from words piled on words a fabric rise,
> He cursed the industry, inertly strong,
> In creeping toil that could persist so long,

And if, enraged he cried, heaven meant to shed
In keenest vengeance on the guilty head,
The drudgery of words the damned would know,
Doomed to write lexicons [dictionaries] in endless woe.

Match the word on the left with its definition.

___1. seethe	a. detest
___2. audacious	b. boring, wearisome
___3. enamor	c. blameworthy
___4. loathe	d. concluding part
___5. reprehensible	e. plan
___6. amity	f. bold
___7. visage	g. boil
___8. epilogue	h. charm
___9. premeditate	i. face
___10. tedious	j. friendship
___11. amiable	k. scold
___12. upbraid	l. friendly

Words in context of *A Midsummer Night's Dream*

Magic still casts its spell on Titania as she tells Bottom,

> Come, sit thee down upon this flowery bed,
> While I thy **amiable** cheeks do coy [caress],
> And stick musk-roses in thy sleek, smooth head,
> And kiss thy fair large ears, my gentle joy.

"**Amiable**" here means "lovely, loveable," slightly different than the modern meaning of "friendly, pleasant." Oberon watches as Titania lovingly strokes and kisses ass-headed Bottom. When Titania and Bottom fall asleep, Oberon says that recently he "did **upbraid**" or scold her for doting on Bottom. He then asked her for the Indian boy which she immediately gave him. Oberon now feels sorry for his queen and releases her from the spell that makes her love Bottom. When she awakes, Titania says,

> My Oberon, what visions have I seen!
> Methought I was **enamored** of an ass.

She then looks upon the sleeping Bottom with whom she was **enamored** or passionately in love and exclaims,

> O how mine eyes do **loathe** his **visage** now.

Titania now **loathes** or hates his **visage** or face. Reconciled with Titania, Oberon says,

> Now thou and I are in new **amity**.

Amity or friendship between Oberon and Titania is restored.

With the arrival of day, Theseus's hunting party comes to the forest and finds the four lovers sleeping near each other. The lovers awake but cannot fully explain what happened. Demetrius then tells Theseus that he no longer loves Hermia and wishes to marry Helena. With this happy resolution to the lovers' problems, Theseus proclaims that the two couples will join him and Hippolyta for a triple wedding ceremony. To complete the happy outcome of events, Bottom wakes up in another part of the woods restored to his normal form and rejoins his friends.

Reflecting on the young lovers' strange story of their night in the woods, Theseus says,

> Lovers and madmen have such **seething** brains....
> The lunatic, the lover, and the poet
> Are of imagination all compact [composed].

The **seething** or agitated minds of lovers, lunatics, and poets all share a surfeit of imagination.

Theseus then asks his director of entertainment what will be the amusement for the evening. The entertainment director lists several options, among which is

> "A **tedious** brief scene of young Pyramus
> And his love Thisbe"....
> A play there is, my lord, some ten words long,
> Which is as brief as I have known a play;
> But by ten words, my lord, it is too long,
> Which makes it **tedious**.

The director says that the play is short but not short enough to prevent it being **tedious** or tiresome. He advises that this play acted by common laborers is not for Theseus. However, Theseus insists on the play. Theseus explains his choice by saying that many great men of learning have come

> To greet me with **premeditated** welcomes,

but out of fear have become flustered and silent.

> Out of this silence yet I picked a welcome,
> And in the modesty of fearful duty
> I read as much as from the rattling tongue
> Of saucy and **audacious** eloquence.
> Love, therefore, and tongue-tied simplicty
> In least speak most, to my capacity.

The great men of learning who came with **premeditated** or planned welcomes became so nervous because of the great respect and admiration they felt for Theseus that their minds froze and they could not remember their lines. Such silence speaks as loudly to Theseus as **audacious** or bold eloquence. Love and tongue-tied simplicity express more than the most sophisticated and elaborate speeches.

Bottom, Quince, and the other workers then perform their play—in all their awkward, blundering simplicity—to the delight of Theseus and his court. As the play ends, Bottom asks Theseus,

> Will it please you to see the **epilogue**, or to hear a ...
> dance between two of our company?

Of course, one most likely "hears" an **epilogue** or concluding speech and "sees" a dance rather than vice versa. Once again Bottom has botched his lines. Theseus selects the dance. After the completion of "Pyramus and Thisbe," a play within the play, Puck concludes *A Midsmmer Night's Dream* by addressing the audience:

> Gentles [ladies and gentlemen], do not **reprehend**....
> Give me your hands, if we be friends.

Puck's lines function as an **epilogue** asking the audience not to **reprehend** or find fault with the play and to show their appreciation by clapping their their hands.

REVIEW EXERCISE
Select the definition closest in meaning.

1. entreat   (a) beg (b) explain (c) scream (d) reward
2. wane   (a) enlarge (b) absorb moisture (c) decline (d) panic
3. disdainful   (a) uncertain (b) scornful (c) happy (d) joyous
4. epilogue   (a) concluding part (b) beginning (c) land (d) sky
5. reprehend   (a) praise (b) capture (c) blame (d) understand
6. flout   (a) scorn (b) introduce (c) depart (d) whip
7. upbraid   (a) support (b) design (c) scold (d) wash
8. audacious   (a) generous (b) stingy (c) noisy (d) bold
9. visage   (a) cemetery (b) prison (c) face (d) castle
10. surfeit   (a) excess (b) deficiency (c) appearance (d) hobby
11. sojourn   (a) soldier (b) visit (c) weapon (d) fortress
12. enamor   (a) escape (b) explain (c) charm (d) renounce
13. premeditate   (a) pray (b) plan (c) anger (d) sing
14. lamentable   (a) sorrowful (b) playful (c) insightful (d) grateful
15. dank   (a) hot (b) cold (c) dry (d) damp
16. amiable   (a) athletic (b) wise (c) careful (d) pleasant
17. seethe   (a) explain (b) disagree (c) boil (d) prepare
18. vexation   (a) praise (b) joy (c) education (d) annoyance
19. prologue   (a) path (b) introduction (c) conclusion (d) sign
20. loathe   (a) collect (b) clean (c) detest (d) congratulate
21. pomp   (a) showy display (b) athlete (c) cruelty (d) gift
22. dissension   (a) agreement (b) disagreement (c) home (d) pain
23. odious   (a) unimportant (b) pleasant (c) helpful (d) hateful
24. preposterous   (a) ridiculous (b) indecisive (c) stern (d) skillful
25. tedious   (a) exciting (b) boring (c) mournful (d) confusing
26. amity   (a) friendship (b) explosion (c) fever (d) enemy
27. extempore   (a) cold (b) hot (c) humid (d) without preparation
28. progeny   (a) parents (b) children (c) enemies (d) friends
29. entice   (a) tempt (b) heal (c) disagree (d) introduce
30. derision   (a) exploration (b) violence (c) ridicule (d) love

8. The Merchant of Venice

mortify
reputed
prodigal
fawn
gratis
spurn
hue
incarnate
impertinent
demure
drone
injunction
prolix
usurer
thwart

gaudy
lewd
obdurate
commiserate
inexorable
impugn
temporal
mitigate
precedent
mercenary
concord
stratagem
paltry
vehement
zeal

Learn these words from *The Merchant of Venice*: Set I

1. ***mortify*** (MOR tuh fy) v. humiliate, shame; discipline one's body and desires through self-denial and self-inflicted punishment
"Mortify" derives from Latin "*mors*" meaning "death." Indeed, when we are mortified by an embarrassing mistake we wish we were dead. "Mortify" also means "punish the flesh" as when Arthur Dimmesdale, the minister in Nathaniel Hawthorne's *The Scarlet Letter*, wears a hair shirt or bristly garment that scratches his skin to atone for his sins. However, Dimmesdale through most of the novel would rather mortify his flesh than make the mortifying or extremely shameful public confession that in an adulterous affair he fathered the child of Hester Prynne, who alone bears the mortification of public exposure. However, the "mortifying groans" that cool the heart in *The Merchant of Venice* illustrate the Elizabethan belief that groans or sighs weakened the heart by depleting it of blood. Shakespeare thus uses "mortifying" in the archaic sense of "killing" that stems from the word's Latin origin meaning "death."

2. ***reputed*** (rih PEW tid—middle syllable rhymes with "cue") adj. generally supposed, thought of, considered
I once discussed with my father Benjamin Franklin's adage that "early to bed and early to rise, makes a man healthy, wealthy, and wise." I asked my father, a gentle scholar who had never manifested any desire for material gain, which of the three attributes—health, wealth, or wisdom—is most important. To my surprise, he said wealth because if you have money it's easier to be healthy and because of your wealth you will be reputed to be wise.

3. ***prodigal*** (PROD ih gul) adj. wastefully or recklessly extravagant, profuse, lavish; n. wastefully extravagant person, spendthrift
Jesus tells the story of the prodigal son, a younger son who demands his inheritance from his father, goes to a foreign land, squanders his wealth, and returns to his father who forgives and welcomes him. The screen star was famous for his prodigal spending on luxury cars, yachts, and private planes. The opposite of a prodigal would be a miser like Scrooge.

4. ***fawn*** (FAWN) v. exhibit affection and show friendliness in the manner of a dog; hence, to seek favor by acting humble, flattering, cringing, and groveling; behaving servilely and obsequiously

The celebrity's wife hated when women fawned over him. Fawning people swarm to the rich, famous, and powerful.

5. *gratis* (GRAT us) adj. & adv. without charge or payment; free
Professors receive gratis copies of textbooks to consider for use in their courses. The idealistic lawyer sometimes worked gratis when she believed in her client's cause and knew that the client could not afford her fee. Banks do not lend money gratis but charge interest.

6. *spurn* (SPURN) v. scornfully refuse or reject
The rebel leader spurned any peace offering that did not grant his people full freedom and independence. Before Romeo met Juliet, he was spurned by Rosaline. When Joseph was a slave in Egypt, he spurned the advances of Potiphar's wife who then falsely accused him of rape.

7. *hue* (HEW, rhymes with "few") n. color, tint
Her colorful dress had all the hues of a rainbow.

8. *incarnate* (in KAR nit) adj. having bodily form; being a living example of; personified, typified; incarnate (in KAR nayt) v. embody in flesh, be living example of
The brutal slave dealer Simon Legree in *Uncle Tom's Cabin* seemed the devil incarnate. Saints incarnate the virtues of their religion. For many, Adolph Hitler is the incarnation (in KAR nay shun) of evil. Hindus believe in reincarnation—that after physical death the soul is reborn in another body.

9. *impertinent* (im PUR tin unt) adj. rude, disrespectful, insolent, impudent; irrelevant
"Pertinent" means "relevant, to the point." In *The Merchant of Venice* the comic character Launcelot Gobbo uses the word "impertinent" when he means to say "pertinent." Thus, instead of claiming that his petition is relevant, he actually says that it is irrelevant, or even worse, impudent and disrespectful. Of course, showing impertinence will not help the granting of one's petition or request. Such a ridiculous or humorous misuse of words is a "malapropism" (MAL uh prop iz um). "Malapropism" derives from the character Mrs. Malaprop in Richard Sheridan's play *The Rivals* (1775). She said such things as "Illiterate [for 'obliterate'] him, I say, quite from your memory." Shakespeare frequently used this comic device long before the word "malapropism" ever entered the English language.

10. ***demure*** (dih MEWR, rhymes with "pure") adj. shy, modest, reserved, coy

Some men find the allure of an innocent, demure woman more seductive than that of someone bolder, more experienced and sophisticated. Of course, "demure" can also mean "pretending to be shy and modest." Only the context of a sentence can tell you whether "demure" conveys true or false modesty.

Working With Words

Complete the following sentences by using each of the following words only once: mortify, reputed, prodigal, fawn, gratis, spurn, hue, incarnate, impertinent, demure.

1. The kindly doctor treated _____ any patient who could not afford a fee.

2. Show some dignity and do not _____ over your boss; he will respect you more.

3. Our coach would never _____ or shame us publicly; he would, however, make us cringe for our mistakes in private conference.

4. When I told the speaker that his remarks were _____ or irrelevant to the topic under discussion, he rudely or impertinently questioned my intelligence and sanity.

5. Grandmother told us that in her day _____ young ladies dressed and acted much differently than today's assertive women.

6. The miser Ebenezer Scrooge in *A Christmas Carol* is Charles Dickens's version of greed _____.

7. The master of the plantation was the _____ father of the great African American abolitionist Frederick Douglass (1817-1895).

8. Even during hard times, the proud couple would _____ offers of charity.

9. We must curb our _____ spending or we will go bankrupt.

10. When Martin Luther King, Jr. said we must judge people by the content of their character and not the color of their skin, he meant that human worth and dignity should not be equated with _____.

Match the word on the left with its definition.

___1. gratis a. modest
___2. hue b. generally supposed
___3. fawn c. having bodily form
___4. mortify d. reject
___5. prodigal e. free
___6. impertinent f. color
___7. reputed g. disrespectful; irrelevant
___8. incarnate h. spendthrift
___9. spurn i. humiliate
___10. demure j. gain favor by flattering and
                    acting humble

Words in context of *The Merchant of Venice*

Set in Italy in Venice and the nearby imaginary city of Belmont, *The Merchant of Venice* is a love story, a portrayal of religious stereotyping, and an exploration of the relationship between justice and mercy. Bassanio asks his best friend Antonio, a wealthy merchant of Venice, for money so that Bassanio can win Portia, an heiress in Belmont. Antonio, his money tied up in overseas ventures, does not have ready cash. To help his friend, the merchant borrows the money from his enemy Shylock, a Jewish moneylender. England had expelled the Jews in 1290. In Shakespeare's time, there were probably less than a few hundred Jews dwelling in England. Therefore, *The Merchant of Venice* illustrates Christian religious prejudices during the Elizabethan period. The outcome of the loan from the Jewish moneylender to the Christian merchant culminates in the most famous courtroom scene in English drama.

As the play opens, Antonio is melancholy but his sadness cannot be attributed to any specific cause. His friend Gratiano tries to cheer him by saying,

> And let my liver rather heat with wine
> Than my heart cool with **mortifying** groans.

Elizabethans believed that the liver warmed by wine would improve the quality of blood and thus make one happy and energetic. Therefore, Gratiano tells Antonio that it is better to have a warm and cheerful flow of blood to keep healthy than to allow oneself to groan which was thought to drain blood away from the heart. Thus, the **mortifying** groans destroy the vitality and can result in death ("**mortifying**" is used here in an old sense of "deadly" rather than in the sense "humiliating"). Gratiano then goes on to say that some men "are **reputed** wise" for keeping silent though they would be revealed as fools if they spoke. They are **reputed** or considered wise only because of their posture of silence. Do not, he tells Antonio, pose as melancholy to be **reputed** thoughtful and profound.

After Gratiano leaves, Bassanio explains that he has been too **prodigal** or wastefully extravagant in his youth and has amassed great debts, mostly to Antonio. If Antonio can just lend him money once more, Bassanio assures the merchant that this time all debts will be paid off. Bassanio feels confident that these funds will enable him successfully to woo Portia—a beautiful, virtuous, and rich lady in Belmont. Only too willing to help his best friend, Antonio says that his entire wealth is on the sea in his merchant ships, but Bassanio can borrow as much as he likes using the merchant's assets as security for a loan.

Bassanio then asks the moneylender Shylock for an enormous loan to be secured by Antonio. As they are talking, the merchant joins them. In an aside, Shylock mutters that Antonio looks "like a **fawning**" or groveling innkeeper and explains that he hates Antonio because "he lends out money **gratis**" or free of interest thus lowering Venetian loan rates. Shylock then asks the merchant why he should lend money to him—a man who has insulted Shylock because of his religion, spit in his face, and kicked him as "you **spurn** a stranger cur" or unfamiliar, worthless dog. The force of the last phrase comes through when one realizes that "**spurn**" literally meant "kick" (as used here) in addition to "scornfully reject." When Antonio says that he is just as likely to spit on and kick Shylock again and Shylock should therefore lend the money as to an enemy rather than a friend so he can feel better about demanding his penalty if the loan is not repaid, Shylock quickly tries to calm the merchant by saying that he would like to be friends and therefore will lend the money without interest. Just for a joke, he asks Antonio to sign a bond that says,

> If you repay me not on such a day,
> In such a place, such sum or sums as are
> Expressed in the condition, let the forfeit
> Be nominated for [stipulated as] an equal [exact] pound
> Of your fair flesh, to be cut off and taken
> In what part of your body pleaseth me.

Bassanio tells his friend not to agree to this bond, but Antonio, confident that his ships will return well before payment is due, willingly seals the bond.

Before Bassanio leaves Venice to reach Portia in Belmont, Portia interviews a suitor, the Prince of Morocco. The prince asks Portia not to dislike him because of his dark complexion. He proudly declares that he "would not change this **hue**" or color of his skin. Portia replies that he stands as fair in her eyes as any suitor that she has yet seen. However, she adds that she has not the power to choose her husband. According to her father's will, a suitor will be presented with gold, silver, and lead caskets. One of these three caskets contains a picture of her. The suitor who chooses the correct casket will marry her.

While Portia leads the Prince of Morocco to the caskets, the scene switches to Venice where Shylock's servant Launcelot tries to decide if he should run away from the moneylender. He reasons that his master "the Jew is the very devil **incarnation**." Launcelot commonly misuses words for comic effect. Here he means to say that Shylock is the devil **incarnate** or the devil embodied in flesh. Having come to this conclusion, he decides to run away.

At this point, Launcelot meets his father who has brought a present for Shylock to insure good relations between his son and the moneylender. Launcelot explains his decision to leave Shylock. When Bassanio comes walking along, Launcelot asks his father to help him get a position with Bassanio. As the father offers his present to Bassanio and starts to plead for his son, Launcelot interrupts and says that his father's request "is **impertinent** to myself," in other words irrelevant and disrespectful. Launcelot, ever the bungler with words, means to say that his father's request is pertinent or relevant to Launcelot himself. However, Bassanio soon understands the request and, because he knows Launcelot well, agrees to hire him.

As Bassanio prepares to travel to Belmont, his friend Gatiano asks to come along. Bassanio says that Gratiano is too wild and unruly; therefore, strangers will find faults in him that his friends overlook. Gratiano promises that he will talk respectfully, carry a prayer book, and "look **demurely**" or modestly when blessings are made at meals. Bassanio agrees that they will go together to Belmont.

Learn these words from *The Merchant of Venice*: Set II

1. ***drone*** (DRONE, rhymes with "phone") n. male bee; loafer, idler; v. speak in a monotonous, dull tone
The non-working male honeybee or drone makes no honey, is stingless, and serves only a reproductive purpose. Hence, we call a parasitic loafer a drone. Since all the idle drone does is buzz, "drone" has also assumed the meaning of dull, monotonous speech or sound. When professors drone, students doze. Excellent teachers who engage in research and constantly hone their communication skills are the antithesis of drones.

2. ***injunction*** (in JUNK shun) n. command or order, especially of a court requiring or prohibiting a specified act
The corporation got an injunction from the court forbidding the workers to go on strike. Portia's suitors in *The Merchant of Venice* must abide by the injunctions laid down by her deceased father before they can be eligible to participate in a guessing game to win her.

3. ***prolix*** (pro LIX) adj. wordy, long-winded, tedious, verbose
The droning of prolix professors induces slumber. Ironically, the prolix Polonius (the Lord Chamberlain in *Hamlet*) says that "brevity is the soul of wit." The editor pruned the prolix writer's sprawling manuscript of one thousand pages to a concise one hundred.

4. ***usurer*** (YOO zur ur) n. one who lends money at an excessive or illegal rate of interest
Shylock in *The Merchant of Venice* is literature's most famous usurer. Medieval Christians regarded lending money at interest as the sin of usury (YOO zoor ee). The Koran, Islam's sacred text, prohibits the taking of interest. Our modern banking system takes interest for granted; the modern financial world considers only excessive or exorbitant interest as usury.

5. ***thwart*** (THWORT) v. block, hinder, frustrate, obstruct
In *The Merchant of Venice* Portia thwarts the moneylender Shylock's plans to cut off a pound of the debtor Antonio's flesh.

6. *gaudy* (GAW dee) adj. tastelessly colorful and showy; garish
When Tod showed up for his first day at work at the funeral home, the director told him that his gaudy outfit better suited a circus, Mardi Gras, or Halloween.

7. *lewd* (LOOD) adj. obscene, indecent, lustful
The censor deleted lewd passages from the book. Puritans think nude is lewd; nudists don't.

8. *obdurate* (OB doo rut) adj. stubborn, unyielding, hardhearted
Neither reason nor tears could alter the views of the obdurate bigot. We associate lions with bravery, deer with speed, and mules with obduracy (OB door uh see) or obdurateness.

9. *commiserate* (kuh MIZ uh rayt) v. feel, express, or show sorrow, sympathy, or pity for; sympathize, condole
Having lost my wife in a car accident, I could commiserate with my neighbor when her husband died of a heart attack. The doctor expressed his commiseration (kuh miz uh RAY shun) when he told me that my mother died. During war we express commiseration and compassion for the losses of our fellow citizens but savor vengeance rather than commiserate with our enemies' sufferings.

10. *inexorable* (in EK sur uh bul) adj. unchangeable or unstoppable by pleading or begging; unyielding
No one can stop the inexorable march of time. Some claim our genes inexorably determine our fate.

Working With Words

Complete the following sentences by using each of the following words only once: drone, injunction, prolix, usurer, thwart, gaudy, lewd, obdurate, commiserate, inexorable.

1. Overprotective parents _____ their children's attempts at independence.

2. To reverse the prodigal and inefficient practices of the company, the new manager began by firing every _____.

3. The bright hues of his _____ outfit contrasted sharply with his fellow workers' conservative gray suits.

4. A word that means "stubborn" and rhymes with "accurate" is
_____ .

5. Disobeying the coach's _____ meant immediate dismissal from the team.

6. When I offered to lend my cousin money above the current rate of interest, he called me a _____.

7. The librarian held a meeting to discuss children's access to _____ material.

8. Although slow to make up his mind, once my father reached a decision he was _____ , unmoved by tears or threats.

9. The _____ speaker droned on and on.

10. Neighbors _____ with each other over their losses of cherished possessions and loved ones during the recent earthquake.

Match the word on the left with its definition.

___1. thwart	a. loafer
___2. lewd	b. moneylender who charges excessive interest
___3. inexorably	c. tastelessly colorful and showy
___4. usurer	d. wordy, tedious, verbose
___5. drone	e. command or order
___6. commiserate	f. obscene, indecent, lustful
___7. prolix	g. unyieldingly
___8. obdurate	h. block, obstruct
___9. injunction	i. stubborn
___10. gaudy	j. sympathize, condole

Words in context of *The Merchant of Venice*

Shylock learns that Launcelot has left to serve Bassanio. The moneylender says that Launcelot eats too much, works too slowly, and sleeps during the day. Shylock states that "**drones** hive not with me." In other words, good riddance to idlers.

Back in Belmont the Prince of Morocco has chosen the gold casket and finds no picture of Portia. He departs. Portia then shows the caskets to her next suitor, the Prince of Arragon. She explains that before selecting a casket the prince must agree to three **injunctions** or commands. He swears to observe:

> First, never to unfold to any one
> Which casket 'twas I chose; next, if I fail
> Of the right casket, never in my life
> To woo a maid in way of marriage; lastly,
> If I do fail in fortune of my choice,
> Immediately to leave you and be gone.

He chooses the silver casket, does not find Portia's portrait, and complies with the third **injunction** by leaving.

In Venice two friends of Antonio discuss the merchant's business ventures. When one of them says he heard the rumor that Antonio lost a ship carrying rich cargo, the other replies, "But it is true—without any slips of **prolixity**...he hath lost a ship." The speaker says he will not be **prolix** or wordy as he confirms the rumor.

At this point Shylock appears. He is distraught, having learned that his daughter Jessica stole his money and jewels and eloped with a Christian named Lorenzo. Shylock's only consolation is Antonio's misfortune: "Let him look to his bond! He was wont to call me **usurer**. Let him look to his bond!" Antonio had called Shylock a **usurer** or one who lends money at an excessive rate of interest. Shylock now threatens that he will demand his pound of flesh if Antonio does not fulfill the conditions of their bond. (An historical note can help us better understand this situation concerning **usury**. Throughout the Middle Ages, Jews had often been excluded from owning land and entering the guilds or professional trade organizations in Christian Europe. Also, the Church during this period regarded the lending of money for interest as immoral. Jewish tradition permitted Jews to lend money at interest to non-Jews. Therefore, since respectable Christians did not lend money for profit and since moneylending was one of the limited opportunities available to Jews for making a living, Jews began to be associated with moneylending and **usury**. By Shakespeare's time, moneylending for profit was in reality also engaged in by Christians, but by now the Jews had been branded with the stigma of **usurer**).

When asked why he would take someone's flesh, Shylock vents his hatred for Antonio,

> He hath disgraced me, and hindered me [stopped me making] half a million, laughed at my losses, mocked at my gains, scorned my nation, **thwarted** my bargains, cooled my friends, heated mine enemies; and what's his reason? I am a Jew. Hath not a Jew eyes? Hath not a Jew hands, organs, dimensions, senses, affections, passions? Fed with the same food, hurt with the same weapons, subject to the same diseases, healed by the same means, warmed and cooled by the same winter and summer, as a Christian is? If you prick us, do we not bleed? If you tickle us, do we not laugh? If you poison us, do we not die? And if you wrong us, shall we not revenge?

Antonio has spoiled Shylock's personal relationships, despised his religion, and **thwarted** or blocked his business deals. But Shylock's speech is more than a list of the merchant's abuses toward him. Shylock also asserts his humanity. Clearly, however, he is the villain of the play. When a Jewish friend informs him that Antonio has lost another ship, Shylock gleefully speculates, "I will have the heart of him, if he forfeit," for with Antonio out of the way, the moneylender's profits will soar.

While Shylock contemplates revenge, Bassanio arrives in Belmont. Portia presents him with the three caskets. Bassanio reasons that attractive ornament often deceptively covers corrupt law, religious error, and imperfections in physical beauty. He concludes that "therefore, thou **gaudy** gold...I will none of thee." He rejects gold and silver as **gaudy** or vulgarly showy coverings that hide defects and selects the lead casket. Portia gives him a ring that she says will preserve their love as long as he keeps it. Gratiano then happily announces that he has successfully wooed Portia's maid Nerissa. Nerissa also gives Gratiano a ring with conditions similar to Portia's. The couples plan to have a joint wedding.

Lorenzo and Jessica then arrive at this blissful scene at the same time as does a letter that dampens the joy. Antonio writes that his ships have all sunk, that Shylock seeks his life to pay the bond, and that Bassanio should come back to Venice to see him before he dies. Portia urges Bassanio to hurry to his friend.

After Bassanio leaves, Portia tells Lorenzo that she and Nerissa will go to a monastery until her future husband returns. Portia asks that Lorenzo manage her house while they are gone. Privately, Portia tells her maid that they will go to Venice disguised as men so that their fiancés will not recognize them. When Nerissa asks,

> Why, shall we turn to men?

Portia answers,

> Fie, what a question's that,
> If thou wert near a **lewd** interpreter!

Portia playfully suggests that Nerissa's remark "shall we turn to men" can mean not only "change into men" but also "sexually approach men" if one gives the phrase a **lewd** or dirty-minded interpretation.

Lightheartedness changes to gravity as Antonio's trial begins in a Venice courtroom. The merchant resignedly prepares to forfeit his life since he knows that Shylock "stands **obdurate**" or unyieldingly hard-hearted. The Duke of Venice, who presides over the court, tells Shylock that Antonio's condition would elicit **commiseration** or sympathy from the stoniest of hearts. Surely, the duke thinks, Shylock will not exact the pound of flesh and, considering the merchant's financial losses, will even accept less money than was borrowed. Shylock remains **inexorable**, unmoved by any pleas.

Learn these words from *The Merchant of Venice*: Set III

1. ***impugn*** (im PUNE—rhymes with "immune") v. challenge as false; cast doubt upon; discredit, gainsay
The prosecuting attorney attempted to impugn the character of witnesses friendly to the defendant in order to cast doubt on their testimony.

2. ***temporal*** (TEM puh rul) adj. pertaining to time; of earthly life, not eternal or spiritual; worldly, secular
The rich businessman astounded everyone by giving away all his temporal possessions and entering a monastery to devote his life to spiritual concerns. Everything material—our bodies, our monuments, even our planet and solar system—is subject to temporal decay and destruction. In the midst of their temporal existence, many human beings long for the infinite and eternal.

3. ***mitigate*** (MIT ih gayt) v. make less severe, intense, or painful; moderate, alleviate, mollify, appease
Judge Loopneck, known as the hanging judge, would never mitigate a sentence no matter how ardently one pleaded for mercy. My employer excused my lateness due to the mitigating circumstances of my sick child, my burglarized home, and my car accident on the way to work.

4. ***precedent*** (PRES ih dunt) n. something said or done earlier that serves as an example, guide, or justification for future action; established practice, custom, convention
When George Washington retired from the Presidency after two terms in office, he set a precedent that no President would run for a consecutive third term; this precedent was upheld until Franklin Delano Roosevelt was reelected for a third and fourth term during World War II. Being the oldest child in my family, I was always told to set a good precedent for my brothers and sisters. The corresponding adjective "precedent" (prih SEED unt) meaning "coming before" is spelled the same but pronounced differently. Dinosaurs, precedent to human beings, ruled the earth.

5. ***mercenary*** (MUR suh ner ee) adj. serving only for money or material reward; n. professional soldier hired to serve in a foreign army
During the Revolutionary War, the British hired German mercenaries called Hessians to fight in America. Of my two close friends, one chose a profession for purely mercenary reasons, disliked it, and left it after a

few years. The other friend, not mercenary at all, devoted himself to sculpture and painting—which he loved—became famous and amassed a fortune.

6. *concord* (KON kord) n. agreement or harmony; peace, amity
The United Nations strives for concord among the countries of the world. Our committee rarely reaches a unanimous decision since our members are seldom in complete concord.

7. *stratagem* (STRAT uh jum) n. deceptive scheme; trick, ruse
When they see a predator near their nest, some mother birds employ the stratagem of feigning an injured wing, tricking the predator to chase them as they draw it away from their nest, always being careful to stay just out of reach. A strategy is a carefully laid out plan, not necessarily employing tricks or deception. However, some strategies do use stratagems, especially in war, to fool the enemy.

8. *paltry* (PAWL tree) adj. ridiculously small, trivial, insignificant, petty, trifling, worthless, contemptible
Quietly under his breath, the waiter cursed the customer—who had pestered him all evening—for leaving such a paltry tip. Many people spend too much time worrying over paltry matters. "Penny wise, pound foolish" means being overly concerned about paltry financial transactions like saving on toothpicks and not giving sufficient thought to large ones like purchasing a car or home.

9. *vehement* (VEE uh munt) adj. showing intense, energetic feeling; passionate, impassioned, ardent, fervid
The congressman's suggestion to raise taxes was met with vehement protest. The angry crowd expressed such vehemence that we feared a riot.

10. *zeal* (ZEEL) n. extreme activity, eagerness, devotion
Young enthusiastic volunteers worked with zeal to get their candidate elected. The zealous (ZEL us) businessman devoted so much time and energy to his company that his neglected wife became jealous. While eagerness and devotion are good, excessive amounts lead to fanaticism, making one a zealot (ZEL ut).

Working With Words

Complete the following sentences by using each of the following words only once: impugn, temporal, mitigate, precedent, mercenary, concord, stratagem, paltry, vehement, zeal.

1. The doctor gave Marilyn some medicine to _____ her migraine headaches.

2. When Charles Dickinson made remarks to _____ the honor of Andrew Jackson and his wife Rachel, Jackson killed him in a pistol duel.

3. When fined $250,000, the billionaire dismissed the penalty as if it were merely a _____ sum.

4. I can appreciate her _____, but I wish her energy and enthusiasm were devoted to a better cause.

5. Although the lawyer did not like the client or the case, she accepted for purely _____ reasons.

6. Only after Romeo and Juliet die do their families belatedly end their feud and finally live in _____.

7. In *The Merchant of Venice*, Portia declares that the spiritual power of God surpasses the _____ power of kings.

8. Is there any previous example or _____ that justifies your action?

9. I used the _____ of burying my son's pill in a spoonful of lime sherbet to get him to swallow his medicine.

10. His reaction was _____ when he stepped in the excrement.

Match the word on the left with its definition.

____1. mercenary   a. pertaining to time; worldly, secular
____2. paltry   b. cast doubt upon; discredit
____3. zeal   c. deceptive scheme
____4. vehement   d. serving only for money
____5. impugn   e. extreme activity, eagerness, devotion
____6. concord   f. insignificant, worthless, trivial
____7. temporal   g. example
____8. precedent   h. harmony; peace
____9. stratagem   i. make less severe; moderate, alleviate
____10. mitigate   j. passionate

Words in context of *The Merchant of Venice*

P ortia, disguised in the manly garb of a lawyer, now enters to defend Antonio. Having studied Shylock's lawsuit, she tells the money-lender that "the Venetian law cannot **impugn** you as you do pro-ceed." His suit cannot be legally **impugned** or challenged and faulted. She asks Antonio if he agreed to the bond, and he admits it. Therefore, says Portia, Shylock must be merciful. When the moneylender asks what compels him to be so, she replies,

> The quality of mercy is not strained
> [cannot be constrained or compelled];
> It droppeth as the gentle rain from heaven
> Upon the place beneath.

She goes on to say that monarchs execute **temporal** or worldly power but that mercy is a quality belonging to God. Therefore, earthly rulers act most like God when they temper justice with mercy. Portia concludes that she has spoken at length "to **mitigate** the justice of thy plea" or soften Shylock's demand for justice. Shylock remains adamant.

Bassanio appeals to the court to make an exception to the law and let him pay the loan amount to release Antonio from the fatal forfeit penal-ty. Portia says,

> It must not be. There is no power in Venice
> Can alter a decree established.
> 'T will be recorded for a **precedent**,
> And many an error by the same example
> Will rush into the state. It cannot be.

If the court bends the law in this case, the act will become a **precedent** or example that will ultimately undermine the Venetian legal system. She once again entreats Shylock to be merciful and offers three times the amount of the loan if Shylock will tear up the bond. Shylock still remains adamant.

Portia then tells Antonio that he must bare his bosom for Shylock's knife. Shylock prepares to cut. But Portia has laid a trap. She points out that the bond says nothing about taking blood. If Shylock draws blood, then everything he owns will be taken by the state according to the law. Shylock now is willing to take Portia's offer of three times the loan amount and let Antonio live. However, Portia will not let him off the hook. He wanted justice so Portia gives him justice. He must take his pound of flesh.

> But just a pound of flesh. If thou tak'st more,
> Or less, than a just [exact] pound...
> Thou diest, and all thy goods are confiscate[d].

Faced with the alternative of either his own death and the confiscation of everything he owns or tearing up the bond, Shylock gives up his lawsuit. However, Portia still does not let him off the hook of the law. She points out that if a foreigner like Shylock has been shown to seek the life of a Venetian citizen—directly or indirectly—the injured party gets half his possessions, the government gets the other half, and the offender dies.

The duke then shows mercy to Shylock by pardoning his life. Antonio also shows mercy by asking the state to return its half of Shylock's wealth and instead let the moneylender pay a mere fine. Furthermore, Antonio says he will give his half to Shylock's daughter Jessica and her Christian husband Lorenzo when Shylock dies. Antonio adds that for Shylock to receive this mercy he must first convert to Christianity and record a document that upon his death Lorenzo and Jessica get all his possessions. Shylock complies.

Bassanio then offers in gratitude to Portia a sum of money equivalent to Antonio's loan. She refuses by saying that her "mind was never...**mercenary**"; she never served only for money. However, she asks Bassanio for the ring that she gave him as a token of her love. Bassanio, not knowing that Portia is the lawyer, at first refuses. When Portia leaves in feigned resentment at the denial of her request, Antonio begs his friend to give her the ring. Bassanio sends Gratiano to give her the ring. When Gratiano presents Portia with the ring, Nerissa, still disguised as the lawyer's male clerk, contrives to get her own ring back from Gratiano.

Back in Belmont on a moonlit night as they await the return of Portia and Nerissa, Lorenzo and Jessica engage in romantic dialogue. Lorenzo extols the power of music on all living things and says,

> The man that hath no music in himself,
> Nor is not moved with **concord** of sweet sounds,
> Is fit for treasons, **stratagems**, and spoils [plundering].

Anyone not responsive to the **concord** or harmony of music is fit for treasonous **stratagems** or schemes and destruction.

Portia and Nerissa then return to Belmont, followed a little later by
Bassanio, Gratiano, and Antonio. Nerissa and Gratiano soon quarrel. In
answer to Portia's question as to the cause, Gratiano says,

> About a hoop of gold, a **paltry** ring
> That she did give me.

This **paltry** or insignificant ring is the ring that Nerissa gave Gratiano to
signify their love. Nerissa says that Gratiano swore with "**vehement**
oaths" or passionate promises that he would wear the ring until his death
and be buried with it in his grave. Gratiano explains to the others how he
gave it to the lawyer's clerk and how Bassanio gave his ring to the lawyer
who saved Antonio. Now Portia feigns anger as she tells Bassanio that if
he had refused the lawyer's request with **zeal** or devotion and determina-
tion, surely the lawyer would not have insisted on taking the ring. Portia
and Nerissa accuse Bassanio and Gratiano of giving the rings to women.
Portia and her maid then say that they will sleep with this lawyer and his
clerk. Antonio intervenes and pledges his life that Bassanio will never
again break faith with Portia. The two women then return the rings to
their suitors to the men's amazement. Portia reveals that she was the
lawyer, Nerissa the clerk, and adds the happy news that three of Antonio's
ships rich with cargo have come safely to harbor.

REVIEW EXERCISE
Select the definition closest in meaning.

1. mitigate   (a) moderate   (b) intensify   (c) criticize   (d) prevent
2. gratis   (a) free   (b) painful   (c) expensive   (d) pleasing
3. obdurate   (a) happy   (b) heavy   (c) unconcerned   (d) stubborn
4. concord   (a) irritation   (b) excitement   (c) agreement   (d) debt
5. zeal   (a) protection   (b) eagerness   (c) joke   (d) mistake
6. incarnate   (a) having bodily form   (b) lost   (c) loving   (d) final
7. demure   (a) flashy   (b) expensive   (c) modest   (d) ungrateful
8. paltry   (a) insignificant   (b) hateful   (c) affectionate   (d) wise
9. impugn   (a) praise   (b) support   (c) frighten   (d) discredit
10. mortify   (a) laugh   (b) prevent   (c) humiliate   (d) deny
11. drone   (a) master   (b) servant   (c) loafer   (d) manual laborer
12. reputed   (a) neglected   (b) supposed   (c) imprisoned   (d) intense
13. vehement   (a) mild   (b) cowardly   (c) greedy   (d) passionate
14. inexorable   (a) unyielding   (b) mistaken   (c) private   (d) angry
15. prolix   (a) concise   (b) wordy   (c) nervous   (d) courageous
16. commiserate   (a) denounce   (b) shame   (c) sympathize   (d) reject
17. impertinent   (a) disrespectful   (b) necessary   (c) polite   (d) hungry
18. mercenary   (a) cold   (b) hot   (c) serving only for money   (d) eternal
19. stratagem   (a) battlefield   (b) business   (c) community   (d) trick
20. injunction   (a) trash   (b) gift   (c) command   (d) nourishment
21. precedent   (a) example   (b) lie   (c) wise saying   (d) administrator
22. fawn   (a) behave servilely   (b) run   (c) sleep   (d) relax
23. prodigal   (a) artist   (b) spendthrift   (c) athlete   (d) pet
24. temporal   (a) happy   (b) worldly   (c) extravagant   (d) passionate
25. spurn   (a) reject   (b) accept   (c) penetrate   (d) lessen a pain
26. usurer   (a) overcharging moneylender   (b) cook   (c) pet   (d) poet
27. thwart   (a) assist   (b) excite   (c) moderate   (d) hinder
28. gaudy   (a) tastelessly colorful   (b) kind   (c) shy   (d) necessary
29. hue   (a) stick   (b) color   (c) friend   (d) poison
30. lewd   (a) natural   (b) comic   (c) obscene   (d) tragic

9. The Tempest

allay	jocund
prerogative	meander
inveterate	travail
extirpate	vigilance
fortitude	muse
prescience	austere
zenith	abstemious
auspicious	abate
importune	ardor
supplant	humane
celestial	penitent
credulous	potent
perfidious	abjure
debauch	remorse
indignity	chastise

Lcarn these words from *The Tempest*: Set I

1. *allay* (uh LAY) v. lighten, relieve, dispel, diminish, calm, pacify, alleviate
"Allay" is to quiet, calm, or relieve such things as pain, doubt, and fear. Medicine allays painful symptoms, assurance allays doubt, and a loving embrace allays a child's fears. John sought to allay his sadness by listening to his favorite music.

2. *prerogative* (prih ROG uh tiv) n. exclusive or special right or privilege
The American writer Ralph Waldo Emerson (1803-1882) said that "a foolish consistency is the hobgoblin of little minds"; evidently he considered it his prerogative to change his mind.

3. *inveterate* (in VET uh rit) adj. firmly established, habitual, deep-rooted
In his autobiographical writings, Mark Twain tells how as children one of his brothers was a model of good behavior while he himself was an inveterate fibber, prankster, and shirker of chores. Inveterate smokers increase their risk of lung cancer. In George Bernard Shaw's play *Pygmalion* (later made into the musical *My Fair Lady*), the speech Professor Henry Higgins is an inveterate or confirmed bachelor.

4. *extirpate* (EK stur payt) v. root out, destroy totally, annihilate, exterminate, eradicate
Legend tells that St. Patrick extirpated the snakes of Ireland. Let us strive to extirpate disease, poverty, and injustice.

5. *fortitude* (FOR tih tood) n. strength or courage in enduring pain or misfortune
Ulysses S. Grant demonstrated his fortitude or bravery as a soldier. Less known is that in the last year of his life and suffering acutely from throat cancer, this impoverished former general and President, in order to provide for his family, wrote his memoirs which he completed just four days before his death—an act of immense fortitude.

6. *prescience* (PREE shee uns, PRESH ee uns, PRESH uns) n. knowledge of events before they occur; foreknowledge, foresight
Some people claim prescience by examining tea leaves, palms, horoscopes, or crystal balls. The adjective "prescient" has similar variants in

pronunciation. In *The Tempest*, Prospero possesses the prescient powers of a prophet.

7. *zenith* (ZEE nith) n. point in the sky directly overhead; highest point; peak, climax, summit, apex
John F. Kennedy and Martin Luther King, Jr. were at their zenith as political and social leaders when they were assassinated. When the old sailor in Coleridge's "The Rime of the Ancient Mariner" describes the blazing heat on his ocean voyage,

> All in a hot and copper sky,
> The bloody sun, at noon,
> Right up above the mast did stand,
> No bigger than the moon,

the sun is at its zenith.

8. *auspicious* (aw SPISH us) adj. favorable, promising a good outcome; propitious
In India, many parents consult astrologers to find out when would be an auspicious date for their children to be married. The ballplayer had an auspicious beginning in the major leagues when in his first turn at bat he hit a home run; however, it was an inauspicious or unfavorable start for his opponent who had just thrown his first major league pitch.

9. *importune* (im POR toon, last syllable rhymes with "prune") v. ask, urge, or beg persistently; repeatedly and insistently entreat
Friends and family of the prisoner importuned the governor to pardon him. However, he would not give in to their importunate (im POR chuh nit) or persistently urgent requests. Shakespeare uses the noun "importunity " (rhymes with "opportunity") when the brother of Hamlet's girlfriend warns her not to

> ...lose your heart, or your chaste treasure open
> To his [i.e., Hamlet's] unmastered importunity.

In other words, he tells his sister not to lose her virginity to Hamlet's unrestrained and insistently pressing demands.

10. ***supplant*** (suh PLANT) v. take the place of (especially by force or scheming), replace, displace, supersede

Electric lights have supplanted candles, automobiles have supplanted horses, and computers have supplanted typewriters. "Supplant" often implies that someone displaces another through force or scheming, as when my supposed friend supplanted me in my girlfriend's affections during my absence. Largely through lies and vicious propaganda, the new dictator succeeded in toppling the old democracy and supplanting the honestly elected president.

Working With Words

Complete the following sentences by using each of the following words only once: allay, prerogative, inveterate, extirpate, fortitude, prescience, zenith, auspicious, importune, supplant.

1. Only a few individuals with special identification passes have the _____ to enter our top-secret laboratories.
2. We told the babysitter not to allow our children to stay up to see the late-night movie on television no matter how much they _____ her.
3. My friend helped to _____ my fears about moving to another city for a new job by telling me that my new position would help my career, that I would make new friends, and that she would frequently visit me.
4. The Sheriff of Nottingham was determined to _____ Robin Hood and his companions from Sherwood Forest.
5. Our grandfather had the _____ to know that the thousand acres of waste land would one day make his descendants wealthy.
6. As the original founders of the company grew old and retired, young executives with different views came to _____ them.
7. I do not believe anything that _____ liar tells me.
8. The American track star Jesse Owens reached his _____ when he won four gold medals in the 1936 Berlin Olympics to disprove Adolph Hitler's views on Aryan racial superiority.
9. The sunny skies, singing birds, and cheerful mood of our children indicated an _____ beginning for our summer trip.
10. She has the _____ to cross the Sahara desert, trek to the North Pole, and climb Mt. Everest.

Match the word on the left with its definition.

____1. zenith   a. favorable

____2. allay   b. courage to endure misfortune

____3. supplant   c. special privilege

____4. prescience   d. relieve

____5. extirpate   e. highest point

____6. inveterate   f. replace

____7. importune   g. habitual

____8. fortitude   h. ask, urge, entrcat

____9. prerogative   i. root out

____10. auspicious   j. foreknowledge

Words in context of *The Tempest*

Twelve years have passed since Prospero, the rightful Duke of Milan (a city in Italy), was overthrown by his ambitious brother Antonio, set adrift with his three-year-old daughter Miranda, and landed on a remote Bermuda island. For the past twelve years Prospero has lorded over this island and its non-human inhabitants with his magic powers. Now, as a ship approaches the island carrying his traitorous brother and others who conspired against him, Prospero magically evokes a powerful storm that threatens to destroy the ship. Thus begins *The Tempest*, a tale of wrongdoing, magic, revenge, and ultimately redemption and forgiveness.

As Miranda, now fifteen years old, witnesses the ship about to be shattered by the raging tempest, she says to Prospero,

> If by your art, my dearest father, you have
> Put the wild waters in this roar, **allay** them.

She pities the terrified men aboard the vessel and asks her father to use his magic arts to **allay** or calm the storm. He assures her that no one will be harmed and then narrates how he and she came to live on this island. All her life on the island Miranda has seen no other human being than her father. The only other island inhabitant visible to her is Caliban, a creature enslaved by Prospero to serve them. Prospero now informs her that he had been the Duke of Milan. Absorbed in intellectual pursuits, he let his brother Antonio handle the practical matters of state while he devoted all his time to his beloved books, especially those on magic. However, Antonio was not content to rule in his brother's name.

> He did believe
> He was indeed the duke, out o' the substitution
> And executing the outward face of royalty
> With all **prerogative**.

Since he exercised the **prerogative** or special privilege of the duke, Antonio thought he was indeed the duke. He therefore conspired with Alonso, the King of Naples (an Italian city), to overthrow Prospero. Antonio would become Duke of Milan and in return would give tribute and allegiance to the King of Naples. Prospero tells Miranda that

> This King of Naples, being an enemy
> To me **inveterate**...

listened to Antonio's plan on how Alonso would "**extirpate** me and mine out of the dukedom" and give it to Antonio. King Alonso, an **inveterate** or deep-rooted enemy of Prospero, agreed to the plan, **extirpated** or rooted out Prospero from his dukedom, and made Antonio Duke of Milan. Alonso and Antonio then set Prospero and Miranda adrift on the sea aboard a rotting boat without sail, rope, or mast. At this point Miranda interrupts her father's story to comment on what a burden she must have been to him aboard this vessel. He replies,

> O, a cherubin [angel]
> Thou wast that did preserve me. Thou didst smile,
> Infused with a **fortitude** from heaven

which enabled him "to bear up against what should ensue." Prospero tells his daughter that she gave him the **fortitude** or courage to endure their hardship. Fortunately, Gonzalo—an old and kindly councilor of King Alonso—had provided the ship with fresh water, food, clothing, and some of Prospero's most prized books. Prospero thus concludes that eventually they drifted to their present island home.

Now that his enemies have been brought to the shores of the island, Prospero says,

> By my **prescience**
> I find my **zenith** doth depend upon
> A most **auspicious** star, whose influence
> If now I court not, but omit, my fortunes
> Will ever after droop.

His **prescience** or foresight tells him that he can be at the **zenith** or high point of his fortune if he acts now because astrologically he is under the influence of a most **auspicious** or favorable star. If he fails to take advantage of this moment, he will lose forever his chance to overcome his enemies and regain his dukedom.

Prospero summons Ariel, a benevolent spirit of the air who inhabits the island and is visible only to the magician. Ariel reports that Ferdinand, the son of King Alonso, was the first to jump overboard, followed by King Alonso and his fellow passengers. Only the crew remained with the ship. Ariel has made sure that King Alonso and his court all reach shore safely and that Ferdinand remains separate from the others. The spirit has brought the ship to harbor and cast a spell to make the crew sleep. Prospero praises Ariel for his service, dismisses him, and then turns to Caliban. Whereas Prospero is airy and benevolent, Caliban—the off-spring of a malevolent witch—is earthy, crude, and savage. Initially, Prospero befriended this creature and taught him language, but Caliban repaid the kindness by attempting to rape Miranda. Since then Prospero has controlled the beast through force and fear. He commands Caliban to bring fuel quickly or he will be plagued by racking pain.

When Caliban leaves to fulfill his chore, Ferdinand wanders into Prospero and Miranda's presence. For Ferdinand and Miranda it is love at first sight. Prospero is pleased. However, Prospero decides to present Ferdinand with obstacles lest he not value Miranda highly because he won her heart so easily. Prospero therefore accuses Ferdinand of being a spy who plans to rule the island. When Ferdinand draws his sword, Prospero's magic overpowers the youth. Miranda with loving sympathy for Ferdinand begs her father to be kind. Prospero pretends that he will treat Ferdinand cruelly, although truly happy that the two young people are in love.

On another part of the island, King Alonso agonizes over the presumed drowning of Ferdinand. Alonso's brother Sebastian adds to the king's tor-ment by saying,

> Sir, you may thank yourself for this great loss....
> You were kneeled to and **importuned** otherwise.

Sebastian reminds Alonso that he was **importuned** or urged not to marry his daughter to the son of the King of Tunis in north Africa. If they had not gone to the wedding in Tunis, they would never have been blown off course and stranded on this island. The good councilor Gonzalo tells Sebastian to soothe rather than scold the grief-stricken king.

The King and his party then fall asleep except for Antonio and Sebastian. Antonio tells Sebastian that they should take advantage of this moment and kill Alonso so that Sebastian can become King of Naples. When Antonio asks if Sebastian agrees with the plan, Sebastian answers,

> I remember
> You did **supplant** your brother Prospero.

Sebastian remembers that Antonio **supplanted** or took the place of Prospero and agrees to kill Gonzalo while Antonio kills Alonso. Once Sebastian becomes king of Naples, he will end the payments that Antonio has been paying Alonso. Just as the conspirators draw their swords, the invisible spirit Ariel wakes the sleepers. Antonio and Sebastian explain that they had heard terrifying roars and raised their swords to protect the king's party.

Learn these words from *The Tempest*: Set II

1. *celestial* (suh LES chul) adj. heavenly
"Celestial" can refer to the sky and heavens. Astrologers study celestial bodies to see how they influence human affairs; astronomers scientifically study the positions, motion, size, and composition of celestial phenomena. "Celestial" can also mean heavenly in the sense of divine or perfect. Tell the chef that his food is celestial, in other words heavenly, perfect, or "out of this world." When the film star Marilyn Monroe married the playwright Arthur Miller, a celestial beauty united with a beautiful mind.

2. *credulous* (KREJ uh lus) adj. too willing to believe; easily convinced; gullible
In Edgar Rice Burroughs's novel *Tarzan of the Apes*, Jane's father—an extremely naive and credulous professor—spends his life savings to buy a treasure map. However, this time his credulity (krih DOO lih tee) pays off because with the help of Tarzan he secures a fabulous fortune.

3. *perfidious* (pur FID ee us) adj. betraying trust; faithless, treacherous
Dante, in his *The Divine Comedy* (an Italian medieval poem that depicts the afterlife), regarded Judas as perfidiously betraying Jesus, and Brutus and Cassius as perfidious betrayers of Caesar. Dante placed these three in his version of Hell for their acts of perfidy (PUR fih dee) or treachery.

4. *debauch* (dih BAWCH) v. lead astray into bad or evil ways; corrupt, seduce
An eighteenth-century novel told a morality tale where an innocent young woman left her country home and was debauched in the big city by drugs, drink, and sex. However, she meets the hero of the story who points out the error of her debauched or unrestrained behavior. Always pure in heart despite her waywardness, she repents her debauchery, marries the hero, returns to the country, and raises a loving family.

5. *indignity* (in DIG nih tee) n. humiliating treatment; offense, insult, or injury to one's self-respect, pride, or dignity
He would rather endure physical torture in private than suffer the indignity of public disgrace. In his "to be or not to be" speech, Hamlet contemplates the indignities or "slings and arrows of outrageous fortune" that make life burdensome.

6. *jocund* (JOK und) adj. merry, cheerful, jolly, jovial
Santa Claus is merry and jocund.

7. *meander* (mee AN dur) v. follow a winding course; wander idly or aimlessly
We meandered leisurely through the countryside exploring different paths and trails. He delivered a long, meandering speech that seemed to have no point. Most often used as a verb, "meander" is also sometimes used as a noun (Shakespeare does so in *The Tempest*) as when describing the meanders or twisting courses of the Mississippi River.

8. *travail* (truh VAYL) n. strenuous, burdensome toil; anguish, agony, tribulation
"Travail" comes from Latin *tripalium,* an instrument of torture with three stakes. Therefore, "travail" suggests very hard, painful labor or hardship. After Hercules in a fit of madness killed his three sons and wife, he atoned for his act through great travail by performing twelve super-human tasks known as the "Labors of Hercules." After Samson revealed the secret of his strength to Delilah, he was blinded and suffered great travail as the Philistines forced him to grind at a mill in prison. Frederick Douglass (1817-1895) wrote eloquently and forcefully about his travails as a slave.

9. *vigilance* (VIJ uh luns) n. alert watchfulness, especially against trouble or danger; wariness
The border guards kept constant vigilance so as not to be surprised by an enemy attack. The vigilant health inspector looked for signs of contami-nated food.

10. *muse* (MEWZ—rhymes with "fuse") n. source of inspiration v. think deeply, meditate, ponder
The Muses were nine daughters of Zeus, the most powerful of the Greek gods. Each presided over her special field such as history, dance, or trag-ic drama. Today, when writers look to their muse, they are trying to find the spirit that inspires them. In our reflective moods, we muse on the grandeur of creation and the meaning of life. In *The Tempest*, Shakespeare uses "muse" as a verb in an old sense that suggests its super-natural origin when he makes a character muse (meaning "marvel or won-der at") appearances and events on an enchanted island.

Working With Words

Complete the following sentences by using each of the following words only once: celestial, credulous, perfidious, debauch, indignity, jocund, meander, travail, vigilance, muse.

1. We observe _____ events such as comets, meteorite showers, and solar eclipses.

2. The heroic knight remained pure and true to his mission despite the efforts of a seductive sorceress and evil magician to _____ him.

3. Shakespeare's King Lear endures much _____ when his wicked daughters dispossess him of his royal benefits and cast him from their homes to wander without shelter in the midst of a horrendous storm.

4. King Lear refers to his _____ or treacherous daughters when he says,

> How sharper than a serpent's tooth it is
> To have a thankless child!

5. We would _____ along the nature trails and observe deer, rabbits, and foxes.

6. The young philosopher loved to _____ on what is beauty, truth, and goodness.

7. My _____ little brother believes anything I tell him.

8. The cheerful music, good food, and lively conversation contributed to the _____ atmosphere at the wedding reception.

9. There is no reason that a poor petitioner has to be treated with _____ by an inconsiderate government official.

10. The lion tamer always maintained her _____ when working with wild animals.

Match the word on the left with its definition.

___1. travail
___2. jocund
___3. meander
___4. celestial
___5. muse
___6. perfidious
___7. credulous
___8. vigilance
___9. indignity
___10. debauch

a. ponder, meditate
b. corrupt
c. betraying trust
d. wander aimlessly
e. humiliating treatment
f. heavenly
g. merry
h. too willing to believe
i. burdensome toil; tribulation or hardship
j. alert watchfulness

Words in context of *The Tempest*

Meanwhile, the butler Stephano and the court jester Trinculo—who became separated from the others during the tempest—meet Caliban elsewhere on the island. Stephano plies Caliban with wine. Impressed with its effects, Caliban exclaims,

> That's a brave god, and bears **celestial** liquor....
> I will kiss thy foot. I prithee be my god.

Caliban thinks only a god could offer such a **celestial** or heavenly drink and offers to worship and serve the drunken butler. Trinculo thinks Caliban

> A most poor, **credulous** monster...a most **perfidious** and
> drunken monster. When god's asleep, he'll rob the bottle.

To Caliban, Stephano is a god; to Trinculo, Caliban is a beast both **credulous** or gullible and **perfidious** or treacherous.

As the three drunks explore the island, Caliban and Trinculo quarrel. Trinculo calls Caliban a "**debauched** fish" The jester sneers at the fishy-smelling and simple-minded Caliban who has been **debauched** or seduced by the wine. When Caliban complains that Trinculo mocks him, Stephano rebukes the jester:

> Trinculo, keep a good tongue in your head....The poor
> monster's my subject, and he shall not suffer **indignity**.

Caliban thanks Stephano for defending him against **indignities** or insults and then unfolds his plan to murder Prospero during his afternoon nap and take control of the island. When the butler and jester approve the plan, Caliban says,

> Thou makest me merry. I am full of pleasure;
> Let us be **jocund**.

Caliban is **jocund** or cheerful as he contemplates the overthrow of Prospero. All this while, invisible Ariel has listened to their conspiracy and flies off to warn Prospero.

In the meantime, King Alonso and his men wearily explore the island. Gonzalo complains, "I can go no further...my old bones aches" as they tread their way through the "maze...and **meanders**" or winding paths of this mysterious land. When the group stops to rest, Antonio draws Sebastian aside and reminds him of their plan to kill Alonso:

> Let it be tonight;
> For now they are oppressed with **travail**, they
> Will not nor cannot use such **vigilance**
> As when they are fresh.

Because the rest of the group are exhausted with **travail** or strenuous toil and therefore cannot be as **vigilant** or alertly watchful as when they are refreshed, Antonio and Sebastian decide to assassinate Alonso that evening.

Unobserved by King Alonso and his men, Prospero watches over them. He magically presents them with a sumptuous feast. Alonso "cannot too much **muse**" or cannot help but ponder in astonishment at this miraculous event. But the famished men no sooner reach for the food then Ariel, in the guise of a harpy (a bird-like monster with the face of a woman), appears amidst flashes of lightning and peals of thunder, claps his wings, and makes the banquet vanish. Ariel then tells Alonso, Antonio, and Sebastian that they will be punished for their crimes against Prospero.

Learn these words from *The Tempest*: Set III

1. *austere* (aw STEER) adj. severe, strict, very plain
The austere martial arts instructor imposed the strictest discipline on his students. His austere manner hid his kind heart. The king left his luxurious place to live a life of austerity (aw STER ih tee) in a monastery.

2. *abstemious* (ab STEE mee us) adj. sparing or moderate in eating or drinking; temperate
When told he must change his eating habits or face premature death, the grossly overweight patient gave up alcoholic beverages and began an abstemious diet of mainly fresh fruit, vegetables, and whole grains. By practicing abstemiousness he regained his health, eventually appeared even trim, and became fond of saying that two-thirds full keeps you healthy while three-thirds full makes the doctor wealthy. To encourage others to eat more abstemiously he also liked to say "moments on the lips, months on the hips."

3. *abate* (uh BAYT) v. reduce, diminish
Only time would abate the grief caused by his wife's death. Bad economic conditions forced the company to fire workers and make salary abatements or reductions.

4. *ardor* (AR dur) n. warmth of feeling; passion, fervor, zeal
At first sight, Romeo and Juliet instantly feel mutual ardor. These intensely ardent or passionate lovers commit suicide for each other. Martin Luther King, Jr. was an ardent advocate for civil rights. My daughter radiates energetic enthusiasm as she ardently works and plays.

5. *humane* (hew MAYN) adj. kind, sympathetic, compassionate, merciful, benevolent
Patients felt comforted by the doctor's humane bedside manner. Buddha was famed for his cool head and warm heart, in other words for his wisdom and humaneness. Unfortunately, human beings do not always act humanely; we often treat fellow humans and animals inhumanely or without kindness and compassion.

6. ***penitent*** (PEN uh tunt) adj. feeling sorry and willing to atone or make up for sin or wrongdoing; contrite
One of the main contributors to *The Oxford English Dictionary* (*OED* for short)—a monumental work that traces the evolution of words—was a madman. Actually, he had been a humane American physician during the Civil War. Later, he suffered from fears of persecution and in England killed a man whom he had mistakingly thought a threat. While serving his life sentence in an English insane asylum, he felt penitent for his act and regularly sent money to help the victim's widow. Throughout his many years in the asylum, he ardently contributed quotations to the editor of the *OED*. His act of penitence or penance helped a poor widow, and his scholarly ardor helped create the greatest of all English dictionaries.

7. ***potent*** (POH tunt) adj. powerful or effective
One drop of the potent venom could kill a dozen people. We found his potent argument convincing. The druggist told us to refrigerate the medicine or it would quickly lose its potency. The negative form of "potent" is "impotent" meaning "powerless, ineffective." Without his sword the samurai warrior felt impotent.

8. ***abjure*** (ab JOOR) v. solemnly give up, renounce, repudiate
When her nurse tells Juliet that she should give up Romeo after he is banished for killing Juliet's cousin, Juliet would rather risk death than abjure Romeo. Richard Wright (1908-1960), author of the novel *Native Son* and the autobiography *Black Boy*, became a member of the Communist Party but later abjured it. Malcolm X (1925-1965) became a disciple of Elijah Muhammad, the leader of the Nation of Islam popularly known as the Black Muslims; after Malcolm made a pilgrimage to Mecca in 1964, he converted to orthodox Islam and abjured Elijah Muhammad and his teachings.

9. ***remorse*** (rih MORS) n. bitter and painful sense of guilt
When the startled dog realized he had accidentally bitten his owner, he felt remorse; for the rest of the day with drooping head and begging for forgiveness, he remorsefully followed his master. "Remorseless" means "without pity or mercy." After being wrongfully imprisoned for fourteen years, the Count of Monte Cristo escapes to pursue remorselessly and to avenge himself on his enemies.

10. *chastise* (chas TYZ) v. punish

The mother grabbed her child as he was about to run in front of a car and chastised him. The chastisement consisted of a severe scolding accompanied by a slap on the behind.

Working With Words

Complete the following sentences by using each of the following words only once: austere, abstemious, abate, ardor, humane, penitent, potent, abjure, remorse, chastise.

1. If you follow your conscience and do what is right, you will not suffer _____.

2. Many of Shakespeare's plays, such as *The Merchant of Venice* and *Measure for Measure*, imply that justice must be tempered with _____ understanding and mercy.

3. Although we feared our _____ teacher who permitted us no behavioral or intellectual slack, to her we owed our future success.

4. Heavyweight champions Joe Louis, Rocky Marciano, and Muhammad Ali could all deliver a _____ knockout punch.

5. We _____ children when they act wrong and praise or reward them when they act right.

6. In his autobiography, Luigi Cornaro, an Italian who lived for approximately a hundred years during the Renaissance, recounts that at forty he was on the verge of death due to an excessively luxurious lifestyle; on the advice of his physicians, he adopted an _____ diet, regained his health, and lived vigorously for about another sixty years.

7. Hamlet's uncle, who killed Hamlet's father, tries to pray for forgiveness but is not truly _____ because he is not willing to give up the kingship for which he murdered.

8. After nearly killing his daughter and himself when driving while intoxicated, he made the decision to _____ alcohol.

9. The medicine caused her fever to _____.

10. Grandmother recalled how in her youth our grandfather courted her with _____.

Match the word on the left with its definition.

___1. humane   a. powerful

___2. austere   b. severe, strict

___3. potent   c. sparing in eating and drinking

___4. remorse   d. repudiate, renounce

___5. chastise   e. sorry and willing to make up for wrongdoing

___6. abstemious   f. reduce, diminish

___7. abjure   g. punish

___8. penitent   h. painful sense of guilt

___9. abate   i. passion

___10. ardor   j. kind, compassionate

Words in context of *The Tempest*

Prospero leaves these men consumed by guilty fear and returns to his daughter and Ferdinand. Assured that Ferdinand has endured enough to prove his love for the young lady, Prospero says to him,

> If I have too **austerely** punished you...
> I tender to thy hand

Miranda. Prospero says that if he has made Ferdinand undergo **austere** or severe trials, he now compensates by offering his daughter's hand in marriage. However, he warns Ferdinand to "be more **abstemious**" or sparing in his physical attentions to Miranda until they are married. The young man assures him that

> The white cold virgin snow upon my heart
> **Abates** the **ardor** of my liver.

Since the liver was thought to be the seat of sexual passion, Ferdinand says that the pureness of his love **abates** or reduces and controls the **ardor** or intensity of his physical desire.

Prospero then conjures the vision of three Greek goddesses to celebrate the wedding of his daughter to Alonso's son. However, he remembers the plot against his life and concludes the performance:

> Our revels now are ended. These our actors
> As I foretold you, were all spirits, and
> Are melted into air....
> We are such stuff
> As dreams are made on [of], and our little life
> Is rounded with a sleep.

Prospero then makes himself invisible as the drunken trio of Caliban, Stephano, and Trinculo come to murder him. Preparing a trap for them, Prospero says of Caliban:

> A devil, a born devil, on whose nature
> Nurture can never stick; on whom my pains,
> **Humanely** taken, all, all lost, quite lost.

Despite all his **humane** or kind efforts to nurture Caliban, Prospero could not change the devilish nature of the creature. Prospero then unleashes spirits in the shape of hounds that drive away the would-be assassins.

After subduing his attackers, Prospero now becomes charitable to King Alonso, Antonio, and Sebastian because

> They being **penitent**,
> The sole drift of my purpose doth extend
> Not a frown further.

Having achieved his purpose by frightening them into **penitence** or sorrow and willingness to make up for their sins, he sends Ariel to release them from their travails. Prospero decides that since his **potent** art of magic has achieved its end,

> This rough magic
> I here **abjure.**

He **abjures** or gives up his **potent** or powerful magic. Ariel then returns with King Alonso and his companions.

Prospero addresses Antonio,

> You, brother mine, that entertained ambition,
> Expelled **remorse** and nature...
> I do forgive thee.

Now that Antonio, who originally showed no sense of guilt when he ousted Prospero, finally feels **remorse**, as do also Sebastian and Alonso, Prospero forgives all three.

At this point Ariel drives in Caliban, Stephano, and Trinculo. Caliban says,

> How fine my master is! I am afraid
> He will **chastise** me.

However, the magnanimous Prospero does not **chastise** or punish Caliban but pardons the three bungling conspirators. Prospero then says that he will leave the island and return with King Alonso and his companions to Naples to celebrate the wedding of Ferdinand and Miranda and then proceed home to Milan.

REVIEW EXERCISE
Select the definition closest in meaning.

1. importune   (a) beg (b) command (c) labor (d) relieve
2. penitent   (a) brave (b) luxurious (c) sorry (d) happy
3. debauch   (a) clean (b) punish (c) corrupt (d) teach
4. vigilance   (a) sleepiness (b) pain (c) watchfulness (d) hunger
5. allay   (a) relieve (b) torture (c) digress (d) persuade
6. credulous   (a) shrewd (b) pleasing (c) painful (d) gullible
7. abstemious   (a) innocent (b) dominant (c) moderate (d) wise
8. austere   (a) gentle (b) funny (c) clever (d) strict
9. chastise   (a) worry (b) forget (c) punish (d) congratulate
10. prerogative   (a) prediction (b) surprise (c) privilege (d) mistake
11. supplant   (a) prosper (b) remember (c) avoid (d) replace
12. celestial   (a) deadly (b) heavenly (c) severe (d) lost
13. jocund   (a) sad (b) lonely (c) jolly (d) burdensome
14. muse   (a) sleep (b) guard (c) destroy (d) ponder
15. remorse   (a) confidence (b) pleasure (c) guilt (d) wisdom
16. abjure   (a) support (b) renounce (c) learn (d) decide
17. perfidious   (a) friendly (b) loyal (c) treacherous (d) proud
18. humane   (a) serious (b) humorous (c) kind (d) violent
19. auspicious   (a) dirty (b) terrible (c) difficult (d) favorable
20. meander   (a) defeat (b) instruct (c) attack (d) wander
21. abate   (a) reduce (b) avoid (c) catch (d) understand
22. indignity   (a) compliment (b) insult (c) promotion (d) escape
23. ardor   (a) passion (b) approval (c) denial (d) boredom
24. zenith   (a) marriage (b) warrior (c) joy (d) highest point
25. extirpate   (a) delay (b) grow (c) destroy (d) travel
26. inveterate   (a) habitual (b) tired (c) unusual (d) spineless
27. travail   (a) hardship (b) laughter (c) adventure (d) reward
28. potent   (a) poisonous (b) ridiculous (c) evil (d) powerful
29. fortitude   (a) enduring courage (b) weakness (c) fear (d) army
30. prescience   (a) ignorance (b) foreknowledge (c) magic (d) skill

10. Word Lists

ROMEO AND JULIET

Key words from plot summaries are in **boldface**.

abhor	conduit	expire	midwife
abound	confound	extremity	mire
absolve	conjure	fathom	mischance
adjacent	consort	feign	misgiving
adversary	constrain	fester	mutiny
adversity	convoy	**fickle**	nimble
affray	cordial	forfeit	nuptial
agile	counterfeit	fray	obscure
aloof	countervail	gall	ordain
ambiguity	crave	gallant	paramour
amble	cull	gape	partisan
amend	dank	**grave**	peevish
antic	denote	grievance	**pensive**
apothecary	descry	harlot	**penury**
apparel	detestable	**heretic**	perforce
apprehend	**dexterity**	hoary	perilous
arbitrate	dire	idolatry	**perjure**
array	**dirge**	impeach	perverse
ascend	discern	importune	prate
aspire	discord	**impute**	predominant
assail	discourse	**inauspicious**	presage
asunder	discreet	inexorable	**privy**
attire	dismal	inter	procure
baleful	dismember	intercession	prodigious
bauble	**disparage**	**inundation**	profess
bawdy	disperse	invocation	prolix
beguile	**dissembler**	kindred	prologue
behest	distill	knave	prompt
bewitch	**distraught**	lamentable	propagate
bier	divine	liege	prorogue
boisterous	doff	loath	**prostrate**
breach	drivel	loathsome	provision
brine	drudge	mangle	purgatory
canker	effeminate	**mar**	purge
carrion	enamored	**martial**	quench
chaste	engross	matron	rail
chide	enjoin	**meager**	**rancor**
choleric	**enmity**	meddle	reconcile
civil	entreat	melancholy	reek

remnant	**scourge**	strew	vanity
renown	seduce	**sullen**	vestal
revel	sententious	sunder	vex
rigor	sepulcher	tarry	vile
rite	sever	temper	visor
rote	shun	transgression	wanton
rouse	sober	tributary	warrant
sallow	solace	unsavory	wax
scant	solemnity	valiant	**wean**
scathe	spleen	valid	
scope	stifle	valor	

MACBETH

Key words from plot summaries are in **boldface**.

abhor	cloister	exasperate	malice
abide	commence	expire	mar
abjure	commend	fatal	marrow
abound	**compunction**	fortify	metaphysical
affliction	concord	fortitude	**mettle**
amend	confound	**fret**	**mirth**
amiss	conjure	fruitless	mortality
antic	consort	gore	muse
antidote	conspire	graft	**niggardly**
appall	constrain	grapple	nonpareil
apparition	continence	grave	oblivious
appease	contrive	guise	obscure
arbitrate	convey	**harbinger**	oracle
attire	**corporal**	hardy	**palpable**
augment	covet	hew	**parricide**
avarice	crave	homage	peerless
bait	credulous	hoodwink	perilous
balm	deft	**husbandry**	pernicious
bane	delinquent	**impede**	perseverance
barren	demerit	imperial	perturbation
beguile	desolate	incense	**petty**
benediction	detraction	incline	pine
bestow	diminutive	**indissoluble**	pious
·bide	**dire**	infirm	plight
blanch	disjointed	initiate	posterity
blasphemous	dismal	integrity	potent
blunt	dispatch	intemperance	prate
bode	distill	interdiction	prattler
bounteous	doff	interim	predecessor
brandish	dolorous	jocund	predominant
breach	dwindle	**jovial**	**pristine**
bruit	eclipse	judicious	prophesy
buffet	ecstasy	lament	prologue
censure	eminence	largess	**prowess**
chafe	entrails	**laudable**	purgative
chastise	entreat	lavish	purge
chide	epicure	lechery	quarry
clamor	**equivocate**	malady	rabble
cleave	esteem	**malevolence**	rancor

233

rapt	salutation	surfeit	valor
ratify	sanctify	surmise	vanquish
raze	scepter	swelter	venom
rebuke	scour	taint	venture
reconcile	scruple	tarry	verity
redress	sear	tedious	voluptuous
reek	sere	teem	vulnerable
relish	sheathe	temperate	wanton
remorse	sieve	thriftless	warrant
rend	solemn	transpose	wayward
repose	solicit	tyranny	weal
requited	staunch	tyrant	wither
resolute	strut	unsanctified	wrathful
rue	subtle	upbraid	yoke
sacrelegious	**sundry**	**usurper**	

HAMLET

Key words from plot summaries are in **boldface**.

aloof	bode	convocation	faction
abate	bounteous	countenance	fathom
abhor	bounty	crave	fawning
abominable	bourn	craven	**felicity**
abridgement	brazen	cudgel	filial
abstinence	breach	dalliance	firmament
access	**brevity**	dally	foil
adhere	broker	**dearth**	forestall
adulterate	buffet	deject	fortify
afflict	bulwark	delve	frank
ambiguous	calamity	dexterity	gape
amble	**calumny**	diadem	gaudy
amiss	canon	dilate	**germane**
anoint	carnal	diligence	glean
antiquity	carouse	dire	grapple
apoplexy	celestial	dirge	gratis
appall	censure	disclose	hallowed
apparel	chaste	discord	harbinger
apparition	chide	discourse	harlot
appurtenance	choler	discretion	harping
ardor	churlish	dismantle	harrow
arraign	**circumscribe**	dismay	havoc
arrant	**circumvent**	distill	heathen
assail	clamor	distract	heraldry
attribute	cleave	divulge	hew
audit	clemency	dole	heyday
auspicious	commencement	ecstasy	homage
awry	commendable	embark	hover
baseness	comply	emulate	hue
batten	conceit	encompass	husbandry
bawd	conception	encumber	hypocrite
bawdy	confound	entreat	imminent
beckon	**conjecture**	**epitaph**	immortal
beguile	conjure	equivocation	impart
behoove	consummation	err	imperious
bellow	contagion	**exhort**	**impetuous**
besmirch	contrive	expostulate	impious
bestial	**contumely**	extant	implore
bestow	conveyance	extremity	import

importune
impotent
incensed
incestuous
inclination
incline
incorporeal
indite
inexplicable
infallible
inhibition
insolence
innovation
insolence
inter
interim
invulnerable
jocund
judicious
knavery
lament
lapse
lecherous
lewd
lisp
loathsome
maggot
maim
malefactor
malicious
mandate
marrow
matron
melancholy
mettle
mirth
mote
mountebank
mute

niggard
obsequious
offal
omen
ominous
palpable
pander
paradox
paragon
parch
pastoral
pate
peevish
perdition
perilous
pernicious
perturb
peruse
pestilent
pious
pith
ponderous
portentous
potent
prate
precedent
precept
primal
privy
probation
prodigal
profane
prologue
promontory
prophesy
purgation
purge
purport
quarry

quintessence
rank
rant
rash
ratify
rebuke
reconcilement
relish
remiss
remorseless
rend
rendezvous
repose
requiem
requite
retrograde
revel
revert
rhapsody
sable
sage
sanctify
sate
satirical
satyr
savory
scant
scourge
scruple
seduce
semblance
shrewd
sinew
solicit
spurn
strumpet
sully
sultry
summit

superfluous
suppliant
surmise
taint
tardy
tedious
temperence
tenable
termagant
thrift
tithe
traduce
tributary
tribute
trivial
truant
turbulent
upshot
usurp
validity
venom
verity
vile
visage
vouchsafe
wanton
warranty
wary
wax
whet
whore
wonted
wrath

JULIUS CAESAR

Key words from plot summaries are in **boldface**.

abide	contagion	gravity	**presage**
abject	corporal	**havoc**	prevail
abridge	**covert**	herald	prodigious
accounter	**covetous**	hurtle	prodigy
affability	crave	**imminent**	proscription
ague	countenance	incense	prostrate
alchemy	cull	**indifferent**	providence
amiss	**cynic**	infirmity	**puissant**
apparel	dank	instigation	purge
apparition	demeanor	**insurrection**	rabble
appease	dint	interim	rash
arbor	disclose	interpose	recount
augur	**disconsolate**	**inter**	**redress**
augment	dismember	knave	reek
awe	disperse	lament	remorse
base	divers	legacy	render
bequeath	earnest	levy	repose
beseech	**emulation**	**loath**	retentive
bestow	**encompass**	luster	revel
bestride	enfranchisement	malice	reverence
blunt	engender	mar	rogue
canopy	enkindle	melancholy	resolution
carrion	entrails	mettle	rite
censure	entreat	mirth	ruddy
chafe	exalt	**misconstrue**	salutation
chastisement	**exigency**	monarch	semblance
chide	exorcist	muse	servile
choleric	expound	mutiny	slander
clamor	extenuate	niggard	sleek
coffer	faction	nimbleness	sober
cogitation	factious	offal	spleen
cognizance	fawn	Olympian	spurn
commend	ferret	oration	strew
concave	firmament	orator	**surly**
confound	fret	ordinance	**tarry**
conjure	gallant	parly	**testy**
consort	garland	peevish	token
conspiracy	**ghastly**	perilous	tributary
construe	gorge	**portentous**	tyrant

unassailable	vaunt	visage	wrangle
underling	venom	**vouchsafe**	wrath
valiant	venture	wary	wrought
valor	vex	whet	yoke
vanquish	vile	wont	

OTHELLO

Key words from plot summaries are in **boldface**.

abhor	chide	engender	imminent
accommodation	choler	ensnare	impediment
adversity	circumspection	ensue	imperious
advocate	citadel	entreat	import
affinity	civil	epithet	importune
affliction	civility	equinox	imposition
alacrity	clamor	equivocal	impotent
amend	commencement	err	impudent
amiss	commend	evade	imputation
amorous	congregate	**extenuate**	incense
anguish	**conjure**	facile	incur
antique	consecrate	fatal	indict
apprehend	**construe**	fathom	indignity
apprehension	contrive	fertile	indiscreet
apt	corrigible	**filch**	**inference**
arraign	credulous	fluster	infirmity
assail	cudgel	forbear	inhibit
balmy	cue	fortitude	**iniquity**
baseness	defunct	frailty	**inordinate**
bauble	delude	frank	insinuating
beguile	**descry**	fulsome	insolent
bereft	despise	gall	interim
beseech	**dilatory**	gallant	kindred
bestial	dire	garland	knave
bestow	**discern**	garner	**lacsivious**
billow	discord	gnaw	languish
bliss	discourse	gratify	lechery
bode	discreet	grave	**lethargy**
bombast	dissemble	gravity	lewd
boon	divine	grievance	liberal
bounteous	dotage	grim	loathe
breach	doting	gross	loll
caitiff	earnest	haggard	maim
carnel	ebb	hallowed	**malice**
carouse	ecstasy	haunt	malicious
castigate	edify	heathen	malignant
censure	**egregious**	homage	mandate
chaste	embark	humane	mangle
cherub	eminent	hypocrisy	manifest

mar
mediator
mettle
minion
misgive
mock
molestation
monumental
mountebank
muse
mutiny
naught
negligence
nether
notorious
nuptial
obsequious
ocular
odious
overt
pagan
palate
palpable
paradox
paragon
parlay
peevish
pelt
penitent
perdition
perjury

pernicious
perplex
pestilence
pilgrimage
pliant
politic
portent
potent
prate
prattle
preposterous
prerogative
procure
profane
profess
prologue
Promethean
propriety
provocation
puny
quirk
rail
rank
rash
rebuke
recoil
reconciliation
redemption
relish
requisite
remorse

reproach
restitution
restraint
revels
rite
rogue
ruffian
ruminate
sanctify
sanctimony
satiety
scant
scion
sensuality
sequester
shroud
shun
slack
slander
smite
solicit
sovereign
speculative
spinster
spleen
sterile
strumpet
subtle
summon
surfeit
surmise

taint
tedious
teem
tempest
timorous
token
traduce
tranquil
trespass
trifle
unreconciled
upbraid
usurp
valiant
valor
vanity
vehement
venial
veritable
vexation
vile
visage
voluble
vouch
wanton
warrant
wary
wrangle
wrath
wrought
yoke

KING LEAR

Key words from plot summaries are in **boldface**.

abatement	conjure	dullard	**incense**
abhor	conspire	**ebb**	incestuous
abjure	contentious	eclipse	incur
abominable	continent	eminence	indignation
adversary	cope	endow	indisposed
affliction	copulation	engender	indiscretion
alight	countenance	enmity	**infirmity**
allay	courtesan	entreaty	ingenious
aloof	covert	**epicurism**	insolent
amity	crave	**equity**	lethargy
amorous	credulous	evasion	loath
ample	dally	exalt	machination
amplify	dearth	**exasperate**	malady
anguish	**defile**	extremity	malediction
antipathy	degenerate	facilitate	malice
apprehension	dejected	fickle	manifest
arraign	depraved	**filial**	manifold
arrant	deride	firmament	mar
array	descry	flay	melancholy
auspicious	detest	foppery	mettle
avouch	diffidence	forbear	mince
balm	**diligence**	frank	mire
bandy	diminish	fraught	misconstruction
beacon	discard	fretful	**miscreant**
beguile	disclaim	gall	monopoly
bellow	discern	gaol	mortify
benediction	discord	glib	motley
beseech	discreet	gorge	mutation
bestow	discretion	grime	negligence
bounty	disdain	**halcyon**	nether
breach	dismantle	harbor	nimble
buoy	disposition	**heinous**	nuptial
carp	dissipation	heretic	obscure
censure	dissolution	hovel	**opulent**
centaur	**dissuade**	illustrious	**ordinance**
chafe	divest	impetuous	pander
chide	dolor	import	parricide
choleric	dominion	importune	**patrimony**
cohort	dotage	impose	pendulous

241

penury
perjure
pernicious
perpetual
persevere
peruse
pestilent
pilfer
pine
pinion
plight
politic
ponder
ponderous
portend
precedent
precipitate
predominance
preeminenece
preferment
pretense
procure
profess
prophesy
propinquity
provision

puissant
quagmmire
queasy
raiment
rash
ravish
reciprocal
reconcile
recreant
redress
relish
remorse
renege
repose
reprieve
reprove
retinue
reverberate
revoke
rigor
roguish
rotundity
rustle
salutation
sapient
savor

scant
scourge
semblance
servile
sever
shun
simper
slack
slipshod
sloth
sojurn
solicit
sot
sovereignty
spleen
spurn
strategem
strife
subdue
superfluous
surfeit
taint
tardiness
tarry
tempest
thwart

tyranny
undivulged
unruly
unsanctified
upbraid
usurp
usurer
valiant
valor
vanquish
verity
vex
vigilance
vile
visage
vouch
vouchsafe
wanton
warp
waywardness
wield
wrath

A MIDSUMMER NIGHT'S DREAM

Key words from plot summaries are in **boldface**.

abate	congeal	gambol	perjure
abide	conjure	gape	pert
abjure	consecrate	grisly	**pomp**
abound	consort	gross	**premeditate**
adamant	contagious	harbinger	**preposterous**
amazon	cue	heresy	prevail
amend	**dank**	hoard	**progeny**
amiable	defile	hoary	prodigious
amiss	**derision**	hue	**prologue**
amity	discord	idolatry	promontory
anon	discretion	impair	purge
antipodes	**disdainful**	impeach	quaint
apparel	disparage	interlude	rail
asunder	dissemble	knave	rash
audacious	**dissension**	**lamentable**	recount
auditor	dole	languish	recreant
austerity	dotage	leviathan	render
avouch	dote	**loathe**	**reprehend**
bacchanal	dulcet	lull	revel
beguile	edict	lurk	rote
bequeath	eloquence	mar	savor
beseech	embark	maze	**seethe**
betroth	**enamored**	melancholy	sentinel
bide	**epilogue**	mimic	sever
bliss	enmity	mirth	shrewd
broach	ensue	mortal	shrewish
celestial	enthrall	mote	shroud
centaur	**entice**	muse	sinister
changeling	**entreat**	nativity	**sojourn**
chaste	exposition	nimble	spleen
chide	**extempore**	nuptial	spurn
churl	extenuate	**odious**	**surfeit**
civil	extort	officious	tarry
clamorous	fawn	orb	taunted
cloister	feign	palpable	tawny
commend	filch	paragon	**tedious**
compass	**flout**	parlous	testy
concord	fray	partition	tyrant
condole	gallant	pelt	**upbraid**

valor	**visage**	wanton	wont
venturous	vixen	warble	wonted
vexation	votary	wax	wrath
vile	**wane**	wend	

THE MERCHANT OF VENICE

Key words from plot summaries are in **boldface**.

abate	**commiserate**	gambol	interrogate
abide	competency	gape	jaundice
abject	coffer	garnish	knave
abridge	**concord**	**gaudy**	knell
accounter	confiscate	gauge	**lewd**
acquit	congregate	giddy	liberal
adversary	conjure	gild	lieu
alien	contrive	glean	lineament
allay	converse	gormandize	livery
aloof	cuckold	**gratis**	loath
amiss	cudgel	gravity	loathe
amity	curb	grievous	malice
amorous	**demure**	gross	manifest
antipodes	devise	guile	mar
appropriation	divers	hazard	meager
attribute	dote	heinous	melancholy
awe	**drone**	heresy	**mercenary**
beget	drudge	**hue**	mirth
beholden	ecstasy	humility	**mitigate**
bellow	edifice	husbandry	monarch
beseech	eloquence	impeach	**mortify**
beset	engender	impediment	nuptial
bestow	entreat	**impertinent**	**obdurate**
bliss	epitaph	importunity	obscure
bounty	excrement	imposition	oration
braggart	exhortation	**impugn**	pagan
burnish	fatal	imputation	pageant
carrion	**fawn**	**incarnate**	palate
chaff	feign	incision	**paltry**
chaste	fledge	incur	peer
cherub	folly	**inexorable**	peevish
cite	foppery	infidel	penance
civility	forfeit	infinite	perjury
clamber	fortnight	infuse	peruse
clime	fray	**injunction**	petty
commend	fulsome	interpose	pied

prate	renowned	strife	**vehement**
precedent	**reputed**	suffice	venture
presage	requite	sunder	viands
privy	rite	superfluity	vile
prodigal	scant	surety	visage
prolix	scepter	taint	wanton
proverb	scruple	tarry	whet
quaint	semblance	tedious	withal
rail	sepulcher	**temporal**	wont
rash	sever	thrift	wrath
ratify	shrew	thrive	wrest
ravenous	shrivel	**thwart**	wrought
recant	slander	treble	yoke
redeem	smug	tribute	**zeal**
remorse	sober	**usurer**	
rend	**spurn**	valiant	
render	**strategem**	valor	

THE TEMPEST

Key words from plot summaries are in **boldface**.

abate	contentious	ignoble	odious
abhor	**credulous**	impertinent	opportune
abide	dalliance	**importune**	oracle
abjure	**debauch**	incense	paragon
abominable	desolate	**indignity**	peerless
abstemious	diffuse	indulgence	**penitent**
abyss	diligence	infirmity	perdition
acquisition	direful	injunction	**perfidious**
advocate	discord	inquisition	pert
affliction	discourse	irreparable	phoenix
allay	discretion	insolent	pied
amend	disperse	**inveterate**	plummet
ample	divers	invert	**potent**
apparition	diversity	invulnerable	prate
ardor	dolor	**jocund**	precedent
ascend	dote	jostle	precept
aspersion	dregs	knave	precursor
auspicious	drollery	knell	**prerogative**
austere	ebb	levy	**prescience**
azure	ecstasy	lieu	prime
barren	endow	loath	profess
bellow	enmity	malignant	promontory
bereft	ensue	manifold	quaint
beseech	entrails	malice	rapt
besiege	entreat	manacle	rash
bestow	expeditious	mar	ratify
blasphemous	**extirpate**	**meander**	recount
bode	felony	mettle	rectify
bounteous	fertile	minion	**remorse**
celestial	flout	mire	repose
chastise	**fortitude**	mischance	reputed
cherub	gallant	mortal	requite
chide	gape	murky	revels
cleave	grave	**muse**	rift
cloven	harpy	mutinous	rite
compassion	homage	nimble	salutation
compensation	hover	nonpareil	sanctimonious
confederate	**humane**	nuptial	savor
conspiracy	indignation	nurture	sever

shroud	tempered	unmitigable	viceroy
sinews	tempest	upbraid	**vigilance**
sloth	tempestuous	urchin	vile
smite	temporal	usurp	vouchsafe
sovereignty	tender	vain	wanton
supplant	throes	valiant	warrant
supple	**travail**	valor	wrangle
surfeit	tribute	vent	wrath
temperance	twain	vex	**zenith**
temperate	tyrant	viands	